Ballet Shoes

Noel Streatfeild was born in Sussex in 1895, one of five children. During her childhood, her father was vicar of St Leonards-on-Sea and later of Eastbourne. She worked in a munitions factory during the First World War and subsequently trained as an actor at the Royal Academy of Dramatic Art in London, acting professionally for a decade before turning to writing. *Ballet Shoes* (1936) was the first of her many novels for children. She won the Carnegie Medal in 1938, and was awarded an OBE in 1983. Noel Streatfeild died in 1986.

Kendall Feaver's plays include *Alma Mater* at the Almeida; *My Brilliant Career* at Belvoir Street Theatre, Sydney; and *The Almighty Sometimes* at the Royal Exchange, Manchester (2015 Bruntwood Prize for Playwriting Judges Award, 2018 UK Theatre Award for Best New Play, 2018 *The Stage* Debut Awards nomination for Best Writer, 2019 Nick Enright Prize for Playwriting and 2019 Victorian Premier's Prize for Drama). Kendall has worked on invited attachments at the National Theatre Studio and the Bush Theatre. She was awarded the 2019 Philip Parsons Fellowship at Belvoir St Theatre, and was part of the inaugural Genesis Almeida New Playwrights, Big Plays Programme in 2019–20.

by the same author

THE ALMIGHTY SOMETIMES
ALMA MATER

KENDALL FEAVER

Ballet Shoes

based on the novel by
NOEL STREATFEILD

faber

First published in 2024
by Faber and Faber Limited
The Bindery, 51 Hatton Garden
London, EC1N 8HN

Published in this revised edition 2025

Typeset by Brighton Gray
Printed and bound in the UK by CPI Group (Ltd), Croydon CR0 4YY

All rights reserved
Play © Kendall Feaver, 2024, 2025
Novel © The Estate of Noel Streatfeild, 1936

Kendall Feaver is hereby identified as author
of this work in accordance with Section 77 of the
Copyright, Designs and Patents Act 1988

Excerpt from *The Children's Hour* by Lillian Hellman,
licensed by permission of Snowball Publishing

All rights whatsoever in this work, amateur or professional,
are strictly reserved. Applications for permission for any use
whatsoever including performance rights must be made in
advance, prior to any such proposed use,
to Casarotto Ramsay & Associates, 3rd Floor, 7 Savoy Court,
Strand, London WC2R 0EX, 020 7287 4450

No performance may be given unless a licence
has first been obtained

This book is sold subject to the condition that it shall not,
by way of trade or otherwise, be lent, resold, hired out
or otherwise circulated without the publisher's prior consent
in any form of binding or cover other than that in which
it is published and without a similar condition including
this condition being imposed on the subsequent purchaser

A CIP record for this book
is available from the British Library

ISBN 978–0–571–39378–7

Printed and bound in the UK on FSC® certified paper in line with our continuing
commitment to ethical business practices, sustainability and the environment.
For further information see faber.co.uk/environmental-policy

Our authorised representative in the EU for product safety is
Easy Access System Europe, Mustamäe tee 50, 10621 Tallinn, Estonia
gpsr.requests@easproject.com

8 10 9

Ballet Shoes was first performed in the Olivier auditorium of the National Theatre, London, on 26 November 2024. The cast, in alphabetical order, was as follows:

Ensemble Stacy Abalogun
Ensemble Eryck Brahmania
Young Juliette Manoff/Ballerina/Ensemble Cordelia Braithwaite
Ensemble Michelle Cornelius
Winifred/Ensemble Sonya Cullingford
Petrova Fossil Yanexi Enriquez
Nana (Miss Gutheridge) Jenny Galloway
Ensemble Courtney George
The Prince/Ensemble Georges Hann
Theo Dane Nadine Higgin
Pianist/Ensemble Nuwan Hugh Perera
Ensemble Philip Labey
Doctor Jakes Helena Lymbery
Ensemble Sharol Mackenzie
Sylvia (Garnie) Pearl Mackie
Katerina Federovsky/Ensemble Xolisweh Ana Richards
Jai Saran Sid Sagar
Pauline Fossil Grace Saif
Great-Uncle Matthew (Gum)/Fidolia/Mr French/Mr Sholsky/ Madame Manoff Justin Salinger
Posy Fossil Daisy Sequerra
Ensemble Katie Singh

All other roles played by members of the company

UNDERSTUDIES
Winifred/Katerina Federovsky Cordelia Braithwaite
Petrova Fossil/Pauline Fossil Courtney George
Nana (Miss Gutheridge) Michelle Cornelius
The Prince Eryck Brahmania
Theo Dane/Doctor Jakes Stacy Abalogun
Sylvia (Garnie) Katie Singh
Jai Saran Nuwan Hugh Perera
Great-Uncle Matthew (Gum)/Madame Fidolia Philip Labey
Posy Fossil Sharol Mackenzie
Offstage Swing Katie Lee
Offstage Swing Luke Cinque-White

Director Katy Rudd
Set Designer Frankie Bradshaw
Costume Designer Samuel Wyer
Choreographer Ellen Kane
Composer Asaf Zohar
Dance Arrangements and Orchestration Gavin Sutherland
Lighting Designer Paule Constable
Sound Designer Ian Dickinson for Autograph
Video Designer Ash J Woodward
Illusions Chris Fisher
Casting Bryony Jarvis-Taylor
Classical Coach Cira Robinson
Dialect Coach Penny Dyer
Voice Coaches Cathleen McCarron and Tamsin Newlands
Associate Set Designer Natalie Johnson
Associate Choreographer Jonathan Goddard
Swing Consultant Eddie Slattery
Fight Director Haruka Kuroda
Staff Director Aaliyah Mckay

Ballet Shoes was revived in the Olivier auditorium of the National Theatre, London, on 25 November 2025. The cast, in alphabetical order, was as follows:

Petrova Fossil Sienna Arif-Knights
Ensemble Julie Armstrong
Jai Saran Raj Bajaj
Ensemble Rosie Boore
Prince/Ensemble Eryck Brahmania
Young Juliette Manoff/Ballerina/Ensemble Chrissy Brooke
Pauline Fossil Nina Cassells
Doctor Jakes Pandora Colin
Swing Stephanie Elstob
Swing Sebastian Goffin
Stage Manager/Ensemble Shailan Gohil
Stage Door Keeper/Ensemble Mark Hammersley
Flyman/Ensemble Georges Hann/Luke Cinque-White
Theo Dane Nadine Higgin
Winifred Gracie Hodson-Prior
Sylvia (Garnie) Anoushka Lucas
Posy Fossil Scarlett Monahan
Ensemble Kaitlyn Moore
Nana (Miss Guthridge) Lesley Nicol
Ensemble Anu Ogunmefun
Swing Suzy Osadchyi
Katerina Federovsky/Ensemble Xolisweh Ana Richards
Ensemble Gabriela Rodriguez
**Great-Uncle Matthew (Gum)/Fidolia/Mr French/
   Mr Sholsky/Madame Manoff** Justin Salinger
Ensemble Katie Singh

All other roles played by members of the company

UNDERSTUDIES
Petrova Fossil Rosie Boore
Jai Saran Shailan Gohil
Prince/Stage Door Keeper Sebastian Goffin
Young Juliette Manoff/Ballerina Gabriela Rodriguez
Pauline Fossil/Winifred Anu Ogunmefun
Doctor Jakes/Nana (Miss Guthridge) Julie Armstrong
Theo Dane/Sylvia (Garnie) Katie Singh
Posy Fossil Kaitlyn Moore
Katerina Federovsky Suzy Osadchyi
**Great-Uncle Matthew (Gum)/Fidolia/Mr French/
 Mr Sholsky/Madame Manoff** Mark Hammersley

Director Katy Rudd
Set Designer Frankie Bradshaw
Costume Designer Samuel Wyer
Choreographer Ellen Kane
Composer Asaf Zohar
Dance Arrangements and Orchestration Gavin Sutherland
Lighting Designer Paule Constable
Sound Designer Ian Dickinson for Autograph
Video Designer Ash J Woodward
Illusions Chris Fisher
Casting Bryony Jarvis-Taylor CDG and Martin Poile CDG
Fight Director Haruka Kuroda
Classical Coach Cira Robinson
Dialect Coach Penny Dyer
Voice Coaches Cathleen McCarron, Zoe Littleton
Associate Choreographer Luke Cinque-White
Associate Lighting Designer Imogen Clarke
Associate Sound Designer Jonas Roebuck
Associate Video Designer Hayley Egan
Associate Illusions Sam Lupton
Staff Director Jasmine Teo

Characters

Pauline Fossil
Petrova Fossil
Posy Fossil
Great-Uncle Matthew (Gum)
Sylvia (Garnie)
Nana (Miss Gutheridge)
Theo Dane
Doctor Jakes
Madame Fidolia
Winifred
Jai Saran
Katerina Federovksy
Mr French
Stage Manager (Albie)
Titania
Oberon
Nick Bottom
The Fly Operator
Mr Sholsky
Arthur (Charles II)
The Clapper Loader
Nikki (The Prince)
Juliette Manoff
A Professional Ballet Dancer
A Stage-Door Keeper

Local schoolchildren, dance-class children,
adult actors, theatre crew, film crew (*etc.*)

Setting

1930s London, but a vibrant fairy-tale version of it.

BALLET SHOES

'. . . a fairy story with its feet halfway on the ground.'
Noel Streatfeild on *Ballet Shoes*

Notes

This script requires a fast, sometimes dizzying pace.
Keep transitions dynamic and engaging –
a hint of magic in every move.

*

Characters often speak over or alongside each other –
no politeness necessary!

A dash (–) signals a brief overlap,
sharp interruption and/or a rapid conversation without space
for breath – your choice.

A forward slash (/) marks the beginning of a longer overlap.

*

Embracing the joy (and athleticism!) of theatre, all cast
members – except those playing Pauline, Petrova, and Posy
Fossil – are encouraged to play multiple roles.

Ideally, the actor playing Gum also portrays Madame
Fidolia, Mr French, Mr Sholsky and Juliette Manoff.

*This text went to press before the end of rehearsals and so
may differ slightly from the play as performed.*

Act One

1. A STAGE, 1919

Great-Uncle Matthew (Gum) – palaeontologist extraordinaire. He delivers a public lecture supported by black-and-white slides.

Gum Fossils. The preserved remains of an ancient plant or animal. From the Latin, *fossilis* – 'dug up, dug out, retrieved from the ground'.

You may think, after a weekend trip to the London Zoo, 'How wonderful! I've now seen almost every animal that has ever walked the earth!' – but that would be stupid because that would be wrong.

Ninety-nine per cent of everything that has ever lived has failed to survive. Eurypterid – gone. The mighty Diplodocus – no more. The last Tyrannosaurus Rex – extremely dead – and sixty-five million years before human beings ever had the chance to witness it.

What remains of that ancient, thunderous lineage?
Just one living relative . . . the chicken.

Sylvia, eleven years old, enters – as yet, unnoticed by Gum. She wears meagre travelling clothes, and carries a paintbox, a suitcase, and a letter.

Everyone has seen a chicken. There is nothing exciting about a chicken. However . . . to unearth the weight-bearing toes of a Troodon . . . or the three-clawed fingers of an Archaeopteryx . . . is to stare directly into the chicken's past . . .

2A. THE FOSSIL-FILLED HOME OF GREAT-UNCLE MATTHEW

Gum and his housekeeper, Alice Gutheridge (Nana), mid-argument. Sylvia, nearby, entertains herself with simple painting supplies.

Nana Her name is Sylvia. Sylvia Rose Brown. Eleven years old. And you, sir, are her last living relative.

Gum Well, there must be some mistake –

Nana The letter is explicit. (*Reading.*) 'Dear Professor Matthew Brown. We, of Bray and Bray and Hopkins, Solicitors, believe you to be the great-uncle of the recently orphaned Miss Sylvia Rose Brown.'

Gum The letter doesn't mention another uncle, does it? A greater uncle? A better uncle? A modest aunt – ?

Nana Sir –

Gum An exceptional cousin, perhaps? A remarkable neighbour – ?

Nana This child is your *family* –

Gum Oh *barely* – a daughter of a daughter of a half-sister I never met –

Sylvia If it would help, I can go to an orphanage?

Gum (*a brilliant solution*) She can go to an orphanage!

Nana Orphanages are for little girls who don't have extremely wealthy great-uncles with half a dozen empty rooms at their disposal –

Gum *Madam.* Those rooms are for my *collections* –

Nana And I have cleaned and dusted those dead and ugly things some twenty-five years, knowing my faith, which was strong when I entered this house, is shaken every time you bring home another creature Our Lord in Heaven failed to mention in the Bible. Now, for the first time, I have the chance to care for something that affirms both my faith *and* my humanity –

Gum There is open paint, Miss Gutheridge! Open paint next to a sixty-five-million-year-old fossil of a baby Tyrannosaurus – !

Nana And lucky you, she made you a picture of it.

Sylvia clasps a painted slide in her hand.

Gum Why? Why would you do that?

Sylvia Your lectures are boring. People pay money to see you talk, and all you're doing is standing on stage in front of boring photographs of boring bones but the bones were once dinosaurs and dinosaurs are *amazing* . . .

Sylvia reveals her artistic impression of how a baby Tyrannosaurus might have appeared in life . . . complete with vibrant feathers.

Gum (*awed*) I agree. You've really captured the giant head, and the tiny *tiny* arms, but no therapod dinosaur should have feathers, Sylvia. It should really look something like a big scary lizard –

Sylvia Are you sure? You said its closest living relative was a chicken. So I thought . . . I thought maybe it looked like a big scary chicken.

Gum studies the picture . . . a very big idea forming.

Gum Interesting . . .

2B. A LETTER, 1920

Gum My darling Sylvia. As expected, your pictures caused a huge stir in New York. Feathers on a dinosaur is a very new idea, and as Miss Gutheridge is only too aware, old ideas are comforting and therefore preferred. But history is not based on facts. History is based on fragments. And every fragment unearthed adds detail and colour to an otherwise-incomplete-picture no one ever thought possible! So, if you'll forgive these long journeys away, I promise: I will find the evidence to prove you *right*. P.S. Don't be alarmed, but on the way to New York, the ship I was travelling on struck an iceberg. I managed to swim to a lifeboat, where I gave a brief but galvanising speech before commandeering the oars to search for survivors. And what do you think I should find, cooing happily, floating on a life jacket in the middle of the ocean . . .

2C. HOME

Sylvia (*delighted*) A baby!

Nana A baby?!

Gum A baby!

Sylvia This is the best present I've ever received –

Nana Are you out of your mind, sir?! You can't gift a twelve-year-old someone else's baby –

Gum What would you have me do, Miss Gutheridge? I looked everywhere for the family; none could be found. The authorities were determined to place her in an orphanage, but I dug my toes in. 'No,' I said, 'the things I find go to my house on the Cromwell Road,' and Sylvia, my darling, you may have the honour of naming her –

Sylvia Pelororhinosauropteryx –

Gum A monstrous-nosed winged lizard – by God, Sylvia, it's *perfect* –

Nana Pauline. Pauline will be her name. The Apostle Paul was rescued from the sea, and I'd much prefer she were named after a blessed saint. Now, I'll get this little one settled, and you and Sylvia can go about clearing the top floor for her nursery –

Gum Miss *Gutheridge* –   **Sylvia** Nana – *no*!

Nana You know the rule. The Professor brings something home, something else has to go . . .

Gum Ugh . . .   **Sylvia** Ugh . . .

2D. A LETTER, 1922

Gum My darling Sylvia. After a year spent excavating a herd of woolly mammoths from the bottom of a glacial ravine, you'll be pleased to know I'm on my way home. P.S. Don't be alarmed, but on the last day of work, I was involved in a small abseiling accident, which required the removal of two fingers and half a leg. P.P.S. While recuperating in a Russian hospital, I made friends with a couple of charming nurses, who kept me 'au courant' with a difficult situation they were facing in the children's ward . . .

2E. HOME

Nana (*holding another baby*) You're mad. That's it, isn't it? You're not just old and English and therefore a little unconventional, you're actually clinically insane –

Gum I'm not going out of my way to find babies, Miss Gutheridge – the babies *persist* in finding me!

Nana We already have a baby. Pauline. Sleeping upstairs in the nursery. And don't you forget our Sylvia, going on fourteen, with a *reputation* to consider –

Gum Don't worry, Miss Gutheridge. Now I know how you feel, I will make other arrangements. Perhaps . . . at an orphanage –

Sylvia Nana, you *wouldn't* – !

Nana Petrova. Her name is Petrova. It sounds a bit like Peter, who was a Holy Apostle, and if we have one baby named after an Apostle, the other should be, too. But no more. Do you hear me, sir? You bring home another baby, I swear to Christ-the-Lord-our-Saviour-O-Him-in-Heaven-and-Earth, I'll give my notice – don't you think I won't . . .

2F. HOME / A LETTER, 1924

Sylvia, now a young woman . . .

Gum My dearest Sylvia, I regret not delivering this personally, but your darling Nana warned me what would happen if I brought home another baby. Therefore, I have delivered this one by district messenger . . .

Nana (*holding another baby*) Oh, this is too much, this is . . .

Sylvia (*reading*) 'The father ran off on the mother, and the mother never wanted a baby on account of her ambitions to dance professionally, so I said to her, "Don't worry, my dear. We already have two babies at home – what's the harm in another?"'

Nana (*ready to explode*) 'What's the harm?' he says . . .

Sylvia (*reading*) 'All the mother had to give the child was a pair of ballet shoes, enclosed. And a name . . . Posy.'

Nana (*exploding*) Posy!

Sylvia (*reading*) 'I know Nana will be upset –'

Nana *Posy* – !

Sylvia (*reading*) '– but there is still the question of a last name, and I'm sure, together, we can find something respectable –'

Nana There's nothing respectable about this little fly-by-night – (*Nonetheless charmed.*) Ohhh blessed lamb . . .

Sylvia (*reading*) 'P.S. Don't be alarmed, my dear, but last week, I was caught in a landslide . . .'

Gum This vast movement of rocks and mud destroyed our lodgings and most of our provisions, but it also revealed the well-preserved edge of something that may, in due course, place our name in the history books. For now, I must remain here to chisel out the rest of it, but when I return home . . . I would be grateful, my darling, for your drawing of it. Always, always, *always* . . . your Great-Uncle Matthew . . .

Sylvia ' . . . Gum.'

Gum disappears.

How long do you think he'll be this time? Two years? Three?

Nana What does it matter? Give the man half a century, he still wouldn't think to send home something practical – bottles, nappies, a potty seat!

She hands the baby to Sylvia.

You go to Sylvia, pet. I'll pick up the essentials.

Nana exits. Sylvia, alone with Posy.

Sylvia Hello, little one. I'm so sorry. You can't be more than three months old, and you already know what it's like to lose a mother. Can I tell you a secret? I know what it's like too. But this is a safe place. And from now on, you won't just survive, my darling . . . you'll *thrive*. I'll make sure of it. Now, come upstairs to the nursery. I want to introduce you to your sisters . . .

3. TRANSITION –
THE LOCAL SCHOOLYARD / HOME, 1934

A rush of whispering, sniggering schoolchildren – coats, satchels, berets – all 1930s story-book charm, though with the hint of a giant schoolyard skirmish just ended.

At home, Nana calls the girls:

Nana Pauline Fossil! Petrova Fossil! Posy Fossil! Kitchen. *Now.*

4. HOME. KITCHEN

Sylvia and Nana are in the middle of preparing the home for new arrivals. The girls stand in front of them: all in disarray, Petrova with her broken toy aeroplane.

Sylvia (*letter in hand*) Expelled?! What – *all* of you – ?!

Posy I didn't do anything, Garnie – it was all Pauline – !

Petrova Don't listen to her, Garnie, it wasn't –

Sylvia Pauline, this is the *third* school. You're supposed to be setting an example for the other two –

Posy Pauline tipped an entire bowl of custard over someone's head –

Pauline Oh shut up, Posy – !

Posy Petrova joined in –

Petrova Shut up, Posy – !

Posy You shut up – !

Nana Why don't you *all* try shutting it for a while –

Sylvia Pauline. Tell me what happened. Please.

Beat.

Pauline One of the older girls asked Petrova why, if we're sisters, we all look so different. So Petrova told them our entire history –

Nana Oh dear – **Petrova** I was just trying to be honest – !

Pauline And another girl said that's exactly the kind of fairytale you'd tell a twelve-year-old when the truth is: our real mother's name is Sylvia Rose Brown, and . . . well, I don't think you really want to know / the rest, so . . .

Nana That's quite enough, thank you –

Pauline If you wanted to make things easier for us, you could try giving us different last names –

Nana Absolutely not. You're all 'P. Fossil'. That's one name, one set of embroidered name-tags –

Pauline But why *Fossil*?! *Fossil* – ?!

Nana Because you chose it – !

Pauline I was five! Who lets a five-year-old choose their own last name – ?!

Posy Hey – why did Pauline get to choose?!	**Petrova** What's wrong with Fossil?

Sylvia Where am I supposed to send you all now? Hm? That was the last school in walking distance –

Pauline Then I guess we won't be going to school –

Sylvia You're going to school –

Nana Or you could send Pauline out to work.

Sylvia Nana . . .	**Pauline** Um . . . *excuse me?*

Nana She's fourteen, Sylvia. That's working age –

Pauline I'm right here, you know – !

Sylvia Nana, that's not an option – Pauline, you're staying in school –

Posy Is that how old you were when you started working, Nana?

Nana I was eleven. And where there isn't money, there isn't choice –

Sylvia Which is why we're bringing in the lodgers –

Pauline Ugh, 'the lodgers' . . .   **Petrova** (*repairing her aeroplane*) Ugh, 'the lodgers' . . .

Sylvia And then when Gum returns –

Nana Faith's a fine thing, Sylvia, but it doesn't pay the milkman –

Sylvia Not now, Nana –

Petrova Are we running out of money – ?

Sylvia No –

Posy Why don't we have any money – ?

Sylvia We're fine! Everything's fine! The lodgers are going to give Nana and I all the money we need to raise you girls properly but those lodgers are due any minute, so right now I need your help moving the last of these fossils –

Petrova We're not getting rid of them, are we – ?

Nana Petrova, a doctor will soon be using this kitchen – how do you think she'll feel eating her breakfast next to a dead, ugly alligator –

Sylvia	**Pauline**	**Petrova**
Deinosuchus Riograndensis, Nana –	Deinosuchus Riograndensis, Nana –	Deinosuchus Riograndensis – and it belongs to Gum – !

Posy Are we going to be living with a doctor?

Nana Yes. A *lady* doctor –

Sylvia Nana, we're being open-minded, remember?

Posy I don't think I want to live with a *lady* doctor –

Petrova I don't want to live with anyone – !

Sylvia It'll be good to have a medical professional living here. Much more useful than that dance teacher . . .

Posy perks up.

Oh . . . oh dear . . .

Posy Is one of the new lodgers a dance teacher?

Sylvia Now, Posy . . . listen to me. When Miss Dane arrives, you're not to overwhelm her –

Posy Are we going to live with a dance teacher – ?

Sylvia Posy –   **Nana** Posy –

Posy Are you telling me we're going to live with a real-life actual dance teacher?!

The doorbell. A moment.
Then Posy races for it.

I'LL GET IT!

5. THEO DANE'S NEW BEDROOM

Theo Dane – a vibrant sunshine-beam of a woman – sits amongst a mess of packing cases, enraptured by Petrova's story.

Petrova Imagine . . . Pauline, as a tiny baby, floating on a life jacket in the middle of an ocean, parents already *drowned* –

Theo *No* –

Petrova I was left at a remote Russian hospital after not one but both of my parents succumbed to a terrible illness –

Theo Oh my –

Petrova Posy is the only one of us with a parent or two that might actually still be living, but her mother had *aspirations* –

Theo Good heavens –

Petrova So Sylvia's not our mother. Not really. She's our guardian – only Pauline couldn't say 'guardian' when she was little so she called her Garnie –

Theo 'Garnie', all right –

Petrova But don't get too comfortable here. Lodgers are strangers, not friends, and Great-Uncle Matthew isn't dead, he's only been missing for ten years, which means he could return at any moment, and then –

We hear Posy before we see her . . .

Posy Miss Dane! Miss Dane! Miss Dane!

Posy arrives, ballet shoes in hand.

Here they are. The most beautiful most important most special things I own –

Petrova If you find her annoying, Miss Dane, just ignore her – that's what we do –

Posy *Petrova* –

Theo They're beautiful, Posy –

Petrova She's always showing off –

Posy I am not – !

Pauline (*entering with fresh linens*) She is though. Always trying on those stupid shoes –

Posy You're both just jealous because you don't have a professional ballerina for a mother –

Pauline You don't know she's a ballerina. She's probably just a chorus girl. Or dancing at the back of some sleazy nightclub –

Theo And what if she is? Don't disparage the chorus, my dear, or nightclubs . . . I, for one, have performed in both!

Posy Have you ever performed in a professional ballet?

Theo No . . . but I've performed just about everywhere else . . .

Theo begins unpacking her suitcases – big signs of a vaudeville past.

First I was 'Baby Cora', then 'Babsy', then 'Tiny Tippy-Toe Tilly' – and when it became obvious there was no longer anything tiny about Tilly, I became 'Miss Winnie Whirl', 'Miss Josie Jive'. I was a singer on a Mississippi gambling boat, a minor role in a major film, and, most recently, 'third-chorus-girl-from-the-left' at the Folies Bergère, where I learnt two very important things: never marry a trumpet player, and hat boxes are a *terrible* place to hide your savings –

Posy So now you teach ballet?

Theo Not just ballet. Drama, elocution, singing, tap, acrobatics, stage combat, everything you need for a life on the stage, including . . .

Theo plays a record on her gramophone.

. . . all the latest dance crazes.

Theo dances . . . something like 'The Big Apple'. Posy, enthralled, copies her.

That's very good, Posy! Petrova . . . would you like to join in?

With a glance at Pauline, Petrova also joins in. The need to move her feet outweighs any allegiance to her older sister . . .

Very interesting footwork, Petrova!

Then Theo approaches the cross-armed Pauline.

Now, Pauline . . . I have one rule, and one rule only . . . When music is playing, you must never *never* stay still!

Now all three sisters are dancing, each enjoying the music in their own unique way.
  But Theo is captivated by Posy.
  Posy, in her element, dances, oblivious.
  The other sisters stop dancing . . . watch Theo watching Posy. Neither Pauline nor Petrova can see anything special in what Posy is doing . . .

> *Suddenly, Doctor Jakes appears – donnish, imperious, very very wet.*

Jakes Well no wonder you can't hear me . . .

But the dancing continues –

I said, NO WONDER YOU CAN'T HEAR ME.

Theo stops the music.

I have been standing – outside – on the street – in the rain – for some fifteen minutes – wondering why no one is answering the front door – which – by the way – is where my life's possessions remain – in increasingly sodden boxes –

Petrova (*shouting up*) GARNIE!

Posy GARNIE!

Petrova NANA!

Posy NANA!

Petrova THE LADY DOCTOR'S / HERE!

Posy THE LADY DOCTOR / HAS ARRIVED!

Jakes Will *every* activity in this house be conducted at the highest possible volume – ?!

Sylvia races in, Nana not far behind.

Sylvia Hello! Hello – sorry – sorry – you must be Doctor Jakes –

Jakes And you are?

Sylvia Sylvia. Miss Sylvia Rose Brown, and this is Miss Gutheridge –

Nana Hello –

Sylvia And these are my –

Jakes Children.

Sylvia Yes. Well. Not mine exactly, but –

Jakes You warned me about the bones and the rocks, Miss Brown. You didn't say I would be living with three children and a grown woman who likes to jump around –

Theo *Excuse me* –

Sylvia Please don't worry, Doctor Jakes – Miss Dane. Miss Dane will be staying here, on the ground floor, in what used to be the dining room – and Doctor Jakes, we've prepared a room for you on the second floor, away from the nursery –

Jakes And the dancing – ?

Sylvia And the dancing.

Nana If you'd like to follow me, Doctor?
　Come on, Fossils. Let's help the doctor with her boxes –

Posy But I want to stay and dance with Theo –

Sylvia Another time. We need to leave Miss Dane to unpack –

Posy But Garnie –

Sylvia Closing the door, Posy! (*Now alone, to Theo.*) Don't be afraid to do that. I've told the girls a closed door means the lodgers don't want to be disturbed – and please, *please* don't worry about the doctor – I suspect she'll keep to herself –

Theo I wanted to talk to you about Posy, actually –

Sylvia Just close the door, Miss Dane – I promise she'll respect it –

Theo She's good. At the dancing, I mean. No training, of course, but from what I can tell, she's been blessed with a natural gift –

Sylvia Oh God, I hope you didn't tell her that –

Theo Well no, but –

Sylvia I've been trying to steer her away from dancing for years –

Theo But why would you / want to?

Sylvia Little girls, all aspiring to be tiny-tutu-wearing princesses, paraded around for an audience of mostly idiot parents to gawk at – who would want to be that –

Theo Me. And I loved it. Earned my own money while doing it too –

Sylvia I don't need her earning money, Miss Dane – she needs to be in school –

Theo (*handing her a brochure*) The Children's Academy of Dancing and Stage Training. Rigorous academic curriculum – performing arts in the afternoon –

Unobserved by Sylvia, Nana re-enters with bath towels for Miss Dane –

Sylvia (*stopping her*) Miss Dane, I . . . Sorry. I'm not sending the child to a school of *performing arts* –

Nana Is there any upfront cost – ?

Sylvia Nana –

Theo Not necessarily. The academy would train her for free, then take a cut when she starts earning money –

Nana And there's a proper education involved – ?

Sylvia Nana – !

Theo Yes, there is. Which happens to include a pliable trade –

Sylvia As dancers! *Dancers!* Nana, this is a house of science!	**Nana** (*after 'dancers'*) They don't need to become *dancers,* Sylvia – they need to be educated.

Theo Oh – oh I'm sorry – sorry. I, uh . . . I was only talking about Posy.

Nana It's a three-for-one deal, Miss Dane.

Theo But are the other girls even interested in going on the stage?

Nana Does it matter?

Theo Well . . . *yes* . . .   **Sylvia** Nana, you can't seriously be considering this –

Nana It's a miracle, isn't it? Any boarding house in London and Miss Theo Dane chooses ours –

Theo There weren't that many options, to be honest with you –   **Sylvia** Oh Nana . . . this is hardly divine intervention . . .

Nana It's a miracle. And I, for one, am eager to walk wherever the waters are divided –

Sylvia (*reading the brochure, unconvinced*) 'The Children's Academy of Dancing and Stage Training –'

Theo, already in the next scene.

Theo A five, six, seven, eight!

6. THE CHILDREN'S ACADEMY OF DANCING AND STAGE TRAINING

Theo leads a class of stage-school students.
The children vary (dramatically) in their ability.
Sylvia, Nana, Pauline and Petrova watch – equal parts fascinated and horrified.
Posy, however, is spellbound.
And then . . . Madame Fidolia enters . . . aloof, mysterious, face caked with stage make-up. She moves with the help of a cane and speaks with a thick Russian accent.
A reverent hush. Theo and the class turn to her . . . curtsy.

Class Madame.

This is too much for Pauline, who heads for the exit –

Pauline No – no – definitely not –

Nana *Pauline –*

Pauline I'm not going here, Nana, you can't make me –

Nana *Stop it – now –*

Pauline This isn't a school, it's a *cult*. A weird dancing *cult* – !

Fidolia You find it strange, child? This class?

Pauline Um . . . yes.

Fidolia Why?

Pauline To start with, no one bows or curtsies to anyone anymore –

Fidolia It is a sign of respect to curtsy to your teacher. A lesson at this academy is never over until you complete your révérence. Winifred, you will demonstrate . . .

Winifred – the academy's star pupil – moves from the front of the class and takes her place on the floor.

We begin in first position . . . then we raise the arms up . . . like so and then we raise them again . . . right . . . left . . . and it concludes with a curtsy . . .

Winifred Madame.

It's beautiful.

Fidolia Which one is Petrova?

Nana pushes Petrova forward.

Petrova I am.

Fidolia You are Russian?

Petrova I was born in Russia.

Fidolia *A ty govorish' po russki?* [Do you speak Russian?]

Petrova doesn't.

(*To Nana.*) You didn't teach the child to speak Russian – ?

Nana What makes you think I know Russian – ?

Fidolia (*to Petrova*) A shame. No matter. You are here now, Petrova, and I will make a good dancer of you, yes?

Petrova is unconvinced.

So this must be Posy Fossil . . .

Posy copies the révérence, ending in an exquisite curtsy.

Posy Madame.

Pauline and Petrova have never hated her more.

Fidolia There is a fine line between confidence and impertinence. Which one are you?

Posy Maybe . . . maybe a little bit scared – ?

Fidolia (*turning to leave*) You will start in the junior classes with Miss Dane –

Posy But Madame –

Fidolia If you work hard, you will progress quickly –

Posy *Madame.*

Posy repeats the dance steps she witnessed in Theo's class – Madame Fidolia rams her cane onto the floor.

Fidolia STOP. You have no training. No technique. You copy, like little bird, but don't yet *understand*. Confidence, Posy Fossil, and the humility to recognise that you always, always, *always* have something to learn.

Madame Fidolia exits. The class immediately relaxes into giggles and gossip.

Nana Did I raise the rudest child in existence –

Posy I wasn't trying to be rude, Nana –

Theo (*to Sylvia*) Here's a list of everything they'll need . . .

Sylvia (*reading the list*) Theo . . . what is this – ?!

Theo I know, I know, it's a lot –

Sylvia Tights, leotards, skirts, shorts, practice dresses, headbands, tap shoes, character shoes, ballet shoes, three pairs *minimum* per child –

Nana Sylvia . . .

The girls are watching . . . Sylvia hides her alarm.

Sylvia We'll buy what we have to buy. And what we don't, we'll make.

7. TRAINING SEQUENCE, VARIOUS PLACES

Music. And we're launched into the middle of the girls' busy new schedule.

Classes begin with Theo. Pauline, Petrova and Posy are all significantly behind. Posy hates being behind. Petrova is in hell. Pauline is bored. And then, in the middle of class, Winifred shows Pauline up. A fire is lit . . . Pauline tries harder.

At home, Nana works at her sewing machine. Sylvia works with a needle and thread. Theo helps the girls improve. Doctor Jakes passes through – a look of utter contempt at the dancing paraphernalia that has now taken over the home.

Off to bed, but the girls are still practicing, all while completing night-time routines.

Posy tries on her mother's ballet shoes. They don't fit. Disappointment. She hangs them back on the wall behind her bed.

As soon as the children hit the bed, they're up again – racing down through the house – collecting new leotards and practice dresses from Nana – past Sylvia who is battling a burst pipe (or some such) – past Doctor Jakes, ready for a morning shower, her anger palpable at this interruption to her morning routine.

At school, the girls complete their everyday maths, English, and science lessons – feet moving under the school desks. Then they take a series of specialist classes: tap, drama, acrobatics, singing, and stage combat. No one volunteers to fight with Pauline.

Back to a ballet class with Theo. Many months have passed. Pauline, Petrova and Posy have all improved. Pauline is capable. Petrova is unhappy and struggles. Posy, however, has become proficient.

Madame Fidolia enters the class and all the children perk up, try a little harder . . . none more so than Posy.

Madame Fidolia watches, expression inscrutable.

The class ends with a beautiful révérence.

Theo Thank you, children. That will be all.

They curtsy.

Children Madame.

The children pack up their things, disperse. Madame Fidolia whispers in Theo's ear.

Theo Winifred, Pauline . . . would you come with me, please?

Winifred and Pauline step forward, confused.
 Posy starts to exit with Petrova, deeply disappointed, and then . . .

Fidolia Posy Fossil? I'd like to see you in my office.

Posy, terrified (and a little excited) follows Madame Fidolia.
 Petrova wanders home, alone, lost in her car magazine. She looks up to see . . .

8. OUTSIDE THE HOUSE

. . . a car. And a man, Jai Saran.

Petrova Is it yours?

Jai Uh . . . sorry – ?

Petrova The 1921 Citroën B2 Torpedo – is it yours?

Jai You know what that is – ?

Petrova How's the suspension?

Jai The suspension – ?!

Petrova How smooth is the ride – ?

Jai Madam, I know what suspension means –

Petrova And?

Jai It's fantastic.

Petrova I knew it!

Jai But this one is over-geared. Too much play in the wheel – too loud. I found it rusting away in a field – but once I rebuild it –

Petrova You build cars – ?!

Jai I fix them. That's the plan, anyway. A few more months driving my boss and his Bentleys around, I'll have enough money to open my own garage –

Petrova Can I sit in the driver's seat – ?

Jai Oh – actually – maybe that's not –

But Petrova is already inside – at the same time, Sylvia hurries out.

Sylvia Petrova . . . Petrova, what are you doing?

Petrova Don't worry, Garnie, I'm not really going to drive it –

Jai Sorry, she uh . . . she just wanted to take a quick look – ?

Sylvia And do you make a habit of loitering outside strangers' houses, inviting little girls to sit inside your car, Mr –

Jai Saran. Jai Saran. And I can assure you, this is a genuine first –

Sylvia Petrova – out of there –

Petrova No, Garnie, this is the first time I've ever sat in an actual car –

Sylvia Petrova, open this door –

Petrova Just one or two minutes longer –

Sylvia Petrova –

Petrova Half a minute longer –

Sylvia Petrova – out – *now*.

Jai Uh . . . I was just driving through when I saw the sign . . .

'Rooms to Let'?

Right now, I'm living above my boss's garage but if you live at work, then you're always working, so . . .

I'm sorry is the room still available, or – ?

Petrova (*to Jai*) You mean you might want to live here?

Jai Well . . . I haven't seen the room yet –

Petrova You have to! You have to live here! Garnie, when you told us we were going to have lodgers, I didn't realise one of them might actually have a *car* –

Jai You'd be getting me too, you know, not just the car –

Sylvia After you see the inside of the house, Mr Saran, I suspect we'll be getting neither.

Jai Well, now I definitely want to see it.

He throws Petrova the keys.

Petrova . . . would you mind watching the car?

Petrova, in awe.

Petrova This is the greatest day of my life . . . *ever*.

9. INSIDE THE HOUSE. AN UNOCCUPIED BEDROOM

Sylvia leads the way. Now it's Jai's turn to be in awe . . .

Jai I've been in the country now for almost six years – two employers, both gave excellent references –

Sylvia I think I need to warn you, Mr Saran –

Jai Jai –

Sylvia Mr Saran. You might not actually enjoy living here?

Jai Why wouldn't I?

Sylvia It's a house full of women. Two of whom are old enough to be your grandmother –

Jai (*pointing to a bird skeleton*) And which one is that?

Sylvia That's a . . . that's a skeleton of a bird, Mr Saran –

Jai No – no, I know –

Sylvia A prehistoric bird – / Palaelodus ambiguus.

Jai I was making a joke – a – a bad joke, obviously – I'm sorry, what did you just call it – ?

Sylvia Palaelodus ambiguus. Its only living relative is the modern-day flamingo –

Jai I might just call him Fred.

Sylvia Actually in this house, we try to use their scientific names, and scientific names only –

Jai Is that what he looked like?

Jai indicates a painting on the wall.

Sylvia Maybe. I wasn't sure . . .

Jai You painted this?

Sylvia I painted all of them.

Jai So you're an artist –

Sylvia No.

Jai A scientist?

Sylvia I repair gauges at the local fuse factory. On weekends, I clean hospital wards. I can also fix a broken boiler, darn a sock, and break up an argument between sisters – but a scientist? No.

Jai What about an illustrator? I would have taken more interest in lessons if my schoolbooks had pictures like these –

Sylvia No one is interested in pictures like these – 'Too scientific to be art, too artistic to be science' – anyway, I don't have time to paint anymore, so –

Jai I think they're extraordinary.

Beat.

Sylvia Look . . . I won't be offended if you don't want the room, Mr Saran –

Jai Did I say that – ?

Sylvia We're having some difficulty shifting it – this house, it's not to everyone's taste –

Jai It's perfect. Fred here is a long way from home. So am I. And I'm not sure Fred has much in the way of close-and-living relatives, so . . .

A moment between Sylvia and Jai . . . a brief shimmer of possibility . . .

I'm sorry, uh . . . What did you say your name was? Mrs –

Petrova, outside, shouts through the front door or up to the window.

Petrova GARNIE! CAN YOU TELL MR SARAN HIS CAR IS STILL HERE?

Sylvia Your car is still here.

Petrova CAN YOU TELL HIM I'M STILL WATCHING IT?

Sylvia She's still watching it.

Petrova CAN YOU ASK HIM: ARE YOU TAKING THE ROOM?

Sylvia Are you taking the room?

Jai If that's okay?

Sylvia (*shouting back*) HE'S TAKING THE ROOM.

Petrova punches the air, dances a bit in excitement. Sylvia and Jai continue to make eyes at each other . . .

10. TRANSITION – THE CHILDREN'S ACADEMY

Posy in a private lesson with Madame Fidolia.

Fidolia And one . . . two . . . three . . . four . . . five . . . six . . . seven . . .

Posy attempts something more difficult, but Madame Fidolia raps her cane.

NO.

The lesson continues.

One . . . two . . . three . . . four . . .

11A. HOME. A HALLWAY WITH A MIRROR

Pauline practises a monologue, script in hand.

Pauline (*struggling*)
Tho speak . . . st . . . a . . . right.
Thou speak . . . *est* . . . aright
I am that merry wanderer of the night
I jest to Oberon and make him smile
When I a fat and bean-fed horse . . . begweely – ?

Doctor Jakes opens her bedroom door – irate.

Jakes Beguile. Beguile. Aright – night – smile – beguile – AA – BB – it *rhymes* –

Pauline Not all of it –

Jakes But that part does.
(*Rapidly, efficiently, but with feeling.*)
Thou speak'st aright;
I am that merry wanderer of the night.
I jest to Oberon and make him smile
When I a fat and bean-fed horse *beguile*,
Neighing in likeness of a filly foal –

Pauline Why do you know it off by heart?

Jakes *A Midsummer Night's Dream.* I taught it for thirty-five years.

Pauline But . . . you're a doctor . . .

Jakes Yes. A Doctor of Literature.

Pauline What's a Doctor of Literature – ?

Jakes First, a few questions for you. One, why are you reciting Shakespeare outside my bedroom door, and two, why are you reciting it so very *very* badly?

Pauline I have an audition. For a West End pantomime. Theo said I should find a classical monologue and then practise it in front of a full-length mirror –

Jakes Why?

Pauline So that I can see what my face and body are doing when I say the words –

Jakes Your face is tight, creased, indignant – your body is tense, rigid, uncompromising – which would be wonderful if you were marching for a fascist dictator –

Pauline Or maybe I just look like this because you're interrupting me –

Jakes Or maybe it's because you don't understand the words.

Doctor Jakes exits into her bedroom.
Pauline, in shock.
Doctor Jakes pokes her head back out.

Well . . . come inside.

Pauline enters the room . . .

11B. BEDROOM OF DOCTOR JAKES

. . . a treasure trove of books, theatre ephemera, photographs . . . signs of a big life, well-lived.
Pauline, despite her best efforts, can't help but be awed.

Jakes Would you like some tea?

Pauline I don't like tea.

Jakes You'll like this one: fresh ginger, maple syrup –

Pauline I don't like either of those things –

Jakes Really. What else don't you like?

Pauline Carrots, peas, tiny yappy dogs, that disgusting dirty-hands feeling of second-hand clothes. Posy – definitely. Petrova – sometimes. Being named after a dead thing you find in a rock –

Jakes Is there anything you do like – ?

Pauline (*the script*) I liked this. Before you ruined it for me.

Jakes What did you like about it?

Pauline I don't know –

Jakes Come on, Pauline, enjoy something, I dare you –

Pauline I like saying the words. I like that they aren't supposed to stay in my head, or . . . on the page. I like making them all . . . I don't know . . . exist?

Jakes And what is the difference, do you think, between simply saying the words out loud and making them *exist* – ?

Pauline (*looking at the door*) Maybe I should go –

Jakes An actress, Pauline, is an archaeologist. She excavates everything hidden beneath the words, and every night, on stage, she exposes those discoveries . . . to the light.

Beat.

Pauline Can I ask you a question now?

Jakes No.

Pauline You've asked me like a million questions already –

Jakes Fine. You can ask me one –

Pauline Who is the woman in all of the photographs?

Jakes Ask me another one –

Pauline Fine. Are you a lesbian?

Beat.

Jakes Do you know what that means?

Pauline The girls at my last school used to call Petrova one behind her back –

Jakes I suspect Petrova is a little too young to know if she's a lesbian or not –

Pauline But you are one? A lesbian, I mean –

Jakes Yes.

Beat.

Pauline Just to be clear . . . I like men. And I'll probably marry one.

Jakes Just to be clear . . . I like women. And you, Pauline, are a child.

Pauline I'm almost fifteen –

Jakes You're a child. With childish concerns. You don't like peas, you don't like dogs, your otherwise loving and supportive guardians lumped you with a last name that you hate – oh boo-hoo –

Pauline I gave it to myself. Actually.

Jakes You chose your own last name – ?

Pauline People usually need one –

Jakes That does tend to be the custom, yes –

Pauline Problem is there were four possibly five babies on my parents' ship when it sank. Only Gum told me the scoundrel captain didn't keep a proper record of his passengers, so I don't know which baby I was or whose baby I was, so I'm nobody. I'm no one. I don't even have a real name –

Jakes You have a name. Best of all, you gave it to yourself. My father gave me my last name, and his father gave it to him – women, in history, forever tied to a long list of grandfathers. But anything you achieve will be attributed to you and you alone – Pauline Fossil, *first* of her name –

Pauline Except I'll never achieve anything –

Jakes No – ?

Pauline I can't do anything, I'm not good at anything –

Jakes There you go again. Depression is the malady of the narcissist, Pauline, and I'm afraid you're one of the worst cases I've ever seen –

Pauline And you're a grumpy old lesbian with too many books and no family who can't afford anywhere better to live than a single bedroom in a stranger's house.

Beat.

Jakes Biscuit?

Pauline takes one.

I did have somewhere 'better' to live. A house – a big, *beautiful* house. Unfortunately for me, it belonged to a woman who wasn't technically legally officially my family, so when she died, it went to her nephew. And when I refused to leave, the nephew told my employer that for the last fifteen years they'd harboured a Sapphic Queer in the English Department. So not only did I lose my partner and my home, I lost my job. None of which did anything to disable my deeply held belief that blood relatives are . . .

She finds herself unable to complete this.

The best kind of family, I think . . . is the kind that you're able to choose.

Doctor Jakes hands Pauline a photograph.

Doris Smith . . . Professor of Mathematics. She was the family I chose.

12. THE CHILDREN'S ACADEMY

Posy, at the barre in flat ballet slippers. Madame Fidolia leads her in a private lesson.

Fidolia . . . and one . . . first . . . to the side . . . and first . . . port de bras to the barre . . .

Posy steps away from the barre.

What are you doing? Why did you stop?

Posy I don't think I should come to these classes anymore.

Fidolia No?

Posy It's not ballet. It's just the same boring exercises over and over and over –

Fidolia Those 'boring' exercises are the foundations of ballet –

Posy I want to go up on my toes –

Fidolia Your technique is no good. The bones in your feet aren't ready –

But Posy is already sliding her mother's pointe shoes on –

Posy Here – just let me show you –

Fidolia *Stop.* You'll hurt yourself. These shoes – they don't even fit.

Posy They fit . . . a little –

Fidolia Are you at home, trying these on – ?

Posy I try them on every day –

Fidolia And I suppose you've also tried to dance in them –

Posy Of course –

Fidolia Then I'm taking them from you –

Posy Madame – *no* –

Fidolia I do not give private lessons so you can undo that work in your bedroom. This is not a game, Posy –

Posy I know, but I –

Fidolia You want these shoes back? You work for them –

Posy But my mother gave them to me . . . They're *mine* . . .

Madame Fidolia, unmoved, places the shoes out of reach. Posy persists.

I've seen the girls in your pointe class, Madame. I'm better than all of them, and . . . and you know it!

Madame Fidolia retrieves a photograph.

Fidolia Do you know who this is?

Posy No.

Fidolia Why would you? You won't find her in any history book.

Posy Why is she holding a chicken?

Fidolia Why indeed. Her name was Katerina Federovsky . . .

A prima ballerina appears, and with her some nebulous sense of turn-of-the century Russia . . .

. . . young . . . beautiful . . . girlfriend of a prince . . . and for a brief moment in time . . . the greatest ballet dancer in the world . . . which made the other dancers feel . . . not so good.

So they conspired against her . . .

First, they unstitched her long skirt so that it fell away, revealing her bare legs. Then, they released live chickens to run across the stage! But Katerina was very good at leaping over chickens – and the audience . . . they demanded those chickens again!

One night, Katerina was told that her greatest part would be danced by a visiting ballerina from Paris . . . Juliette Manoff. And Juliette Manoff was very famous, yes, but Juliette Manoff was also thirty-four years old, which meant, in ballet terms, that Juliette Manoff was a wrinkled old bat.

Katerina flew into a violent rage. What could this wrinkly old bat Manoff teach Katerina Federovsky, young, beautiful, girlfriend of a prince, but Posy . . . when Manoff had finished dancing . . . the tears . . . they *ran* down my face –

Posy *Your* face –

Fidolia They *ran* down Katerina's face. It was the most beautiful performance she had ever seen . . .

The prima ballerina disappears . . .

Katerina begged Juliette Manoff to teach her: 'Please – I want to learn to do what you do!' And you know what Manoff said . . . ?

Posy What? What did she say?

Fidolia 'Return to the barre and complete your boring exercises –'

Posy Oh Madame – !

Madame Fidolia raps her cane.

Fidolia Back to work, Posy . . . and one . . . first . . . to the side . . . (*Etc.*)

Posy stares longingly at her mother's shoes as Madame Fidolia walks them away.

13. A STAGE

Winifred sings the opening song from a new production of Alice in Wonderland. *It's a sweet little tune, which Winifred sings with surprising power. She complements it with some skilful (but extremely cutesy) ballet.*
Behind her a row of 'Alices' assemble – all similarly dressed, complete with a hair ribbon. Pauline, in the mix, wears her own version of an Alice-dress, hair ribbon also in place. Winifred's attire pales in comparison.

Winifred (*singing, as Alice*)
She tells a tale, filled with history's turn,
With a lesson to grasp and a moral to learn
But the sun's so warm, and the river's so clear
And the grass is full of daisies, and the daisies . . .

Mr French, the play's director, appears.

Mr French (*spoken, script in hand, as Alice's sister*) Alice! Daisies belong in the ground, they're not to be plucked and turned into a necklace.

Winifred (*monologue, to the audience*) You know, my sister often tells me, 'Alice, stop dreaming. The real world is right in front of you.' But her world has books with no pictures and no conversations, and the world I want to find is . . .
(*Singing, chorus.*) Beyond the page, beyond the sky
Deep beneath the earth, out the other side
Where late is on time, and time is . . . a lie
That's my Wonderland
My Wonderland –

Mr French (*as the sister, interrupting*) Alice!

Winifred (*singing, dreamily, cheekily, to the audience*)
. . . in Wonderland.

Winifred finishes . . . a quick révérence . . . then returns to the line.

Mr French Thank you, Winifred. Delightful as always. Could I have Pauline Fossil, please?

Pauline steps forward.

Would you like to sing, dance, recite, or, perhaps, like your fellow Fidolian, you'd like to attempt a charming mix of all?

Pauline Um . . . I'd . . . uh –

Mr French Quickly, please –

Pauline I'd like to recite?

Mr French Which page – ?

Pauline Oh, um . . . I've prepared a different monologue? From a modern play?

Mr French Oh dear . . .

Pauline takes a moment to centre herself. She conjures Doctor Jakes, who appears – separately – to coach her.

Jakes Breathe, Pauline. Try to remember the meaning beneath every word.

Pauline snaps up – adjusts her gait. A strong Pennsylvanian accent emerges from her mouth as she takes on the role of twenty-two-year-old Karen from Lillian Hellman's The Children's Hour.

Pauline (*as Karen*) Martha is dead.
So last night you found out you had done wrong to us. And now you have to right that wrong or you can't rest your head again. Well, don't rest it. I won't be your confessor. Take your conscience some place else, get somebody else to help you be a 'good' woman again.

You told us that night you had to do what you did. Now you have to do this. A public apology and money paid and you can sleep and eat again. You and all those who always know how right they are. What's somebody else's life to you? A way to show your own righteousness. And if you happen to be wrong, then you can always put it right some other day.

She gestures suddenly to Winifred –

I have a dead friend! Get out of here . . . and be noble on the street.

Pauline drops out of character . . . waits for instruction.

Mr French Right. Interesting. Well, let's hope you can also sing and dance, Miss Fossil – have you prepared the required song?

As the line of disappointed Alices disperse, Pauline begins to sing and dance

Pauline (*singing, as Alice*)
She tells a tale, filled with history's turn,
With a lesson to grasp and a moral to learn –

Winifred remains, stares at her new competition in horror.

14. A GARAGE

Jai and Petrova (both in grease-covered overalls) are repairing the car.

Petrova (*demonstrating*) This is a piqué passé. Piqué passé is mostly what I'm doing when I'm the back-end of the caterpillar.

Jai That's very impressive, Petrova –

Petrova It's not really. Theo said if I could learn to smile, I'd be just as good as the others, but all I can think about is how much I hate it . . .

Jai Then maybe you should think about something you love –

Petrova (*perhaps dancing*) Clearing out a carburettor and greasing the leaf springs –

Jai There. You'll be starring in a West End pantomime in no time.

Petrova Jai . . . do you think if you're one thing when you're twelve, when you're older . . . you can be something else?

Jai I don't see why not.

Petrova Do you think a girl could work in a garage?

Jai I know one who already does . . .

Petrova What about fly an aeroplane?

Jai Amelia Earhart? Amy Johnson?

Petrova Amelia Earhart and Amy Johnson probably had rich parents who paid for their flight lessons –

Jai What about Bessie Coleman?

Petrova Who?

Jai Bessie Coleman? Queen Bess? Bessie Coleman didn't have rich parents – Bessie Coleman grew up working in the cotton fields. And when the flight schools in America refused to teach her, Bessie Coleman taught herself French, then set sail for Paris . . .

Petrova Well maybe I can go to Paris and learn from Bessie Coleman –

Jai Well, not from her, but . . . one of the others, maybe . . .

Petrova Why not Bessie?

Jai Bessie, uh . . . oh God, I don't actually know how to explain this –

Petrova She's dead, isn't she? How did she die? Was it an aeroplane accident –

Jai Death is not . . . Petrova, death is not something you need to think about at your age –

Petrova Do you want to know how long it takes for a dead thing to turn into bones?

Jai Um, actually, I'm not sure I do –

Petrova When I was little, I asked Gum, and Gum said, 'Two to six years, depending on conditions,' so if Bessie Coleman died, and it was more than six years ago, then –

Jai Petrova, I . . . Is this something you're worried about? Death, I mean?

Petrova No . . . Yes . . . Sometimes? Mostly I just worry all the choices about who I am and what I can do have sort of been made for me already . . .

Jai That's not necessarily true –

Petrova Please *please* don't say something soppy like –

Jai 'All you need is a dream – just follow your dreams – if you dream it, you can be it –'

Petrova Exactly –

Jai I would never. Dreaming isn't real. Dreaming is something you do with your eyes closed. So, when I was your age, I made a vow. To keep my eyes open. To see and take whatever opportunity presents itself –

Petrova Like what – ?

Jai Fixing old bicycles . . . broken clocks . . . tending the wireless on a boat to Singapore . . . three long years in Malaya, which, to be honest, I'd rather forget –

Petrova But now you're here. Living in the best house in the world –

Jai That's true –

Petrova Fixing a car you own –

Jai In a garage I own –

Petrova So that means you'll stay? For a while, at least – ?

Jai I hope so. (*Gestures to start the car.*) But if this doesn't work, I'll try something else. And again. And again if I have to. There's always an opportunity to change course, Petrova . . . you just have to look for it . . .

The car sputters, then roars into life. Petrova, delighted.

Petrova Can you teach me how to drive?

Jai Maybe. When you're older –

Petrova What about now? We won't go straight on the main roads, obviously –

Jai Obviously –

Petrova But we could find a country lane? Or a field? Or an empty beach – ?

Jai Petrova –

Petrova Don't worry, Jai. Posy knew she was a good dancer before she had a single lesson, and that . . . is exactly how I feel about driving.

15. A THEATRE DRESSING ROOM

Pauline practises her lines, revelling in her new role. Winifred, nearby.

Pauline 'Who in the world am I? Ah, that's the great puzzle. I knew who I was this morning, but I've been so many people since then –'

Winifred The line is, 'I've changed so many times since then.'

Pauline It's close enough.

Winifred Mr French will expect you to get it right.

Pauline Mr French told me I'm the greatest little actress he's ever discovered –

Winifred I've been working since I was four. I'm a better singer. And dancer –

A Stage Manager (Albie) pokes their head in.

Stage Manager Miss Fossil – the crew need you in position –

Pauline I'll be there shortly, thank you –

Stage Manager Miss Fossil –

Pauline (*sweet, but firm*) Thank you!

Pauline makes no effort to leave. Turns to Winifred.

Winifred . . . I've been meaning to have a little talk with you. It seems strange to have you lounging around in my dressing room when you could be – oh I don't know – polishing my shoes or collecting my wrap from backstage –

Winifred I'm not your maid, Pauline –

Pauline No, but it really is *exhausting* being the star of a *major* professional production –

Winifred For you, this is fun, right? A hobby? For me, this is a job, and I'm getting half of what you get to learn everything you do, but if I didn't take this job, my little brothers and sisters . . . we don't eat –

Pauline My family doesn't have any money either –

Winifred Liar. You came to that audition in a brand-new dress –

Pauline My Nana made it for me –

Winifred You came in a car! With a chauffeur – !

Pauline He's our lodger – he lives with us – !

The Stage Manager reappears, more desperate.

Stage Manager Miss Fossil –

Pauline (*snapping*) Yes, *thank you*!

Pauline gathers her things.

Winifred, if you're going to keep talking to me like this, I might need to ask Mr French for my own dressing room –

Winifred No . . . You wouldn't dare –

Pauline Oh I'm sure he'll understand. The lead actor can't be expected to share with an understudy as *insufferable* as you –

Winifred shoves Pauline.
Pauline shoves her back.
Alternatively, Winifred blocks the door or pulls at Pauline's skirt to stop her.
Regardless, both tumble into a scuffle – their respective Alice costumes making this a difficult task. It plays more farce than fight, but Pauline, sharper, scrappier, quickly gains the upper hand.
At the same time, Mr French approaches with the Stage Manager.

Mr French Never in my *life* have I had to ferry an actress from her dressing room! Albie, where in the Labyrinth of Knossos are we – ?

Stage Manager Here, sir –

Mr French (*knocking, opening the door*) Miss Fossil, I –

Mr French takes in the scene.

Albie. Put the other actors on tea break. Make it a long one.

16. TRANSITION – HALLWAY, HOME

Nana, Doctor Jakes and Theo are gathered around a locked bathroom door. Posy, somewhere nearby, practises ballet.

Nana Pauline! Unlock this door, please!

Jakes Pauline, listen to me. You don't have to open the door –

Jai enters with Petrova.

Nana Oh yes you do – !

Jai What's going on?

Jakes Nana, everyone is entitled to a locked bathroom door and a little mournful solitude.

Theo Pauline locked herself in the bathroom.

Jai Do you want me to . . . I don't know . . . maybe I could try and break the door down, or . . . ?

Posy (*hearing 'break the door down'*) Oooh, fun!

Petrova (*hearing 'break the door down'*) Can I help – ?

Theo PAULINE, MR SARAN IS GOING TO BREAK THE DOOR DOWN!

Sylvia arrives with her toolbox.

Sylvia All right, everyone. Move aside.

Sylvia expertly removes the lock.

Pauline, I'm coming in . . . and it's just me, no one else . . .

The others start to back off . . . but not completely. Sylvia enters; closes the door behind her.

17. BATHROOM

Pauline, fully clothed, in the empty bathtub. The sink tap is running.

Sylvia Is that so they think you're having a bath?

Pauline It's so no one can hear me crying.

Sylvia Ah. Clever. Usually, I just hide myself in the linen cupboard, but that . . . that could work too.

Sylvia turns the tap off.

What happened, sweetheart . . . ?

Pauline Nothing.

Sylvia Are you nervous about playing Alice?

Pauline I'm not Alice –

Sylvia Don't say that. Doctor Jakes and Miss Dane both told me you're absolutely perfect for her –

Pauline I am. I know everything about her. I've excavated every single line and it doesn't matter, because Mr French gave the part to Winifred.

Sylvia And . . . was that . . . unexpected or – ?

Pauline Winifred told Mr French I tried to strangle her with her own costume –

Sylvia Did you – ?

Pauline Obviously not that well if she survived to talk about it!

Sylvia Did Winifred say something? Something . . . unkind – ?

Pauline refuses to answer, storms through –

Pauline It's too late to find another understudy, so they've offered me that at least, but Garnie . . . how do I go back there tomorrow – ?

Jakes (*from behind the door*) TELL HER A PROFESSIONAL THEATRE ACTRESS WOULD – !

Sylvia (*opening the door*) Right. Downstairs. All of you. Now.

Sylvia closes the door.

I'm not going to tell you what to do. I've been trying to do that since you were a baby. It's never worked. I suspect because you've never liked anything enough for me to threaten you with its removal –

Pauline So now, as punishment, you're going to stop me from going to any more auditions –

Sylvia As long as you want to go, Pauline, I'll take you.

It's a powerful thing . . . discovering something you enjoy. It helps you endure everything else in life that's impossible to avoid. Grief. Disappointment. Bills, taxes, mind-numbingly boring day jobs –

Pauline Is that what painting does for you?

Sylvia doesn't answer the question. Instead, she wraps an arm around Pauline, kisses the top of her head, then moves to leave . . .

Sylvia I'll talk to Mr French tomorrow. If Winifred behaved badly, there's no reason she should have the part and not you –

Pauline It was my fault too. If I'm being honest, Garnie . . . it was my fault more than it was hers.

Sylvia processes this.

Sylvia Then this is a hard lesson to learn –

Pauline But everyone will know! Tomorrow, at the theatre, everyone will be talking about me –

Sylvia Let them. You have a job to do. For the next six weeks, you are going to be a kind and conscientious understudy. Which isn't such a terrible thing to be, because for the next six weeks, you'll still be in a theatre. So use this time. Watch. Enjoy. *Learn.*

18. OPENING NIGHT – *ALICE IN WONDERLAND* PRODUCTION

A White Rabbit appears, removes a watch from his waistcoat pocket . . .
  Pauline moves towards him, but the White Rabbit looks past Pauline to Winifred . . . who appears in full Alice costume.
  Winifred chases the White Rabbit . . .
  . . . down a rabbit hole . . .

. . . and into an extravagant Christmas-pantomime-Wonderland, complete with a chorus of pantomime children, adult actors in the lead roles.

The scenes shift quickly, each highlighting Petrova's discontent: one part of a dancing caterpillar's tail, a dancing teapot, a dancing playing card (etc.).

In the middle of the action, Petrova appears to pause production and conjure a small moment of personal 'Zen': Jai teaches her how to drive a car . . . which may or may not correspond to her dancing . . .

Jai Ready, Petrova? First, press the clutch pedal all the way down.

Petrova (*echoing*) Left foot, clutch pedal, all the way down.

Dancer 1 (*whispering to another dancer*) What is she doing?

Jai Shift the gear lever to first.

Petrova (*echoing*) Shift, lever, first.

Dancer 2 I can't keep count, Petrova!

Jai Steady on the wheel – hands ten to two – / Petrova, wait . . . Petrova . . . *slow down!*

Petrova Release the clutch – press the accelerator – and – !

Dancers *Petrova.*

Petrova, big smile on her face, is now having an almost bearable time.

 But Winifred, on stage, struggles to remember her next line . . .

Winifred 'This is . . . this is . . . um . . .'

Noticing her distress, from backstage, Pauline whispers the line –

Pauline 'This is nonsense! Can't you be more straightforward?'

Winifred (*as Alice*) 'This is nonsense! Can't you be more straightforward?'

Mad Hatter 'But Alice . . . then you'd miss all the twists and turns!'

The dance resumes.
   Winifred slips offstage to thank Pauline – evidence of a growing friendship.
   Just as the scene reaches some sort of apex, it retreats, dissolves as if part of a dream . . . revealing, in its wake . . .

19A. KITCHEN

. . . the kitchen, decorated for Christmas Eve. Merriment, silliness, celebrations abound.
   Doctor Jakes sings a Christmas carol, loudly and drunkenly.
   Beneath this, Posy cheekily bounds about, parodying the dancing she's just witnessed . . .

Posy Pas de chat is meant to be like a cat, but Tweedledum was pas de cow, pas de dog, pas de elephant – !

Pauline Posy . . .   **Petrova** You don't even know, Posy –

Theo Drinks, drinks, drinks – does everyone have a drink in their hand?

Posy Doctor Jakes has two.

Jakes It's Christmas Eve, Posy. There are different rules for Christmas Eve.

Nana (*drink in hand*) I quite agree, Doctor –

Jai (*impressed*) Nana –

Jakes Bottoms up, Nana – down the hatch – !

Theo Wait – wait – a toast! Someone – please – a toast!

Jai To Petrova!

All To Petrova!

Jai The greatest dancing playing card and caterpillar tail there ever was!

Jakes And to Pauline!

All To Pauline!

Jakes The best Alice we *never* saw!

All The best Alice we *never* saw!

Theo Whether you continue on the stage or not, little Fossils, may you always remember the feeling of warm lights on your face, abject terror in the pit of your stomach, and the heavenly *heavenly* hush before it begins . . .

Jakes (*in religious agreement*) . . . Ohhh the lights . . .
 . . . Oh, I used to *love* the terror . . .
 Ah . . . the hush . . . . . .
the heavenly *heavenly* hush!

Sylvia (*whispering to Jai*) What the hell are they talking about – ?

Jai I have absolutely no idea –

Nana All right, Fossils! Christmas Eve tradition. One present each from under the tree –

| **Petrova** There's so many this year . . . | **Posy** I want the biggest . . . Which one's the biggest . . . ? | **Pauline** Stop pushing me, Posy! |

Theo (*a parcel*) Let's start with this! Addressed to 'The Fossil Family'. It was caught up in my own mail – I've never seen so many stamps – !

Sylvia, seeing the parcel (*and all its stamps*), *cries out suddenly – covers her mouth in shock.*

Petrova It's from Gum, isn't it?

Pauline Can we open it, Garnie – ?

Sylvia No – wait –

19B. A LETTER, 1927

Gum appears, still legendary, but very alone, and looking a little worse for wear . . .

Gum My darling Sylvia. By the time this package arrives, it will be Christmas. Which Christmas of which year, I can't be certain, but I've been assured by the captain of a passing whaling ship that it will arrive for at least one of them. Enclosed are presents for the babies. Turquoise, blue-green stone of the ancients, for Pauline. Seed pearls, salvaged from an oyster farm, for Petrova. Red coral, the skeletal remains of a tiny marine animal, for Posy. And for you, Sylvia . . . the fulfilment of an old promise. P.S. If, for any reason, this letter is my last . . .

19C. KITCHEN

Sylvia (*reading*) '. . . I want it to be known and publicly understood . . . that the significant scientific discovery . . . as shown in these photographs . . . must be credited entirely to Sylvia Rose Brown.'

Sylvia, distressed, trying not to show it . . .

Posy Does this mean Gum is coming home soon?

Sylvia passes the letter to Nana to show her the date.

Pauline Garnie . . . are you all right – ?

Sylvia It's bedtime.

Nana Pauline, Petrova – you have a matinee tomorrow. Posy, you should have been in bed hours ago –

Pauline But Nana – **Petrova** Nana – **Posy** No – Nana!
Nana Bedtime. Now.

Nana exits with the girls.
From the lodgers, 'Goodnight, Fossils,' 'Well done,' etc.
Sylvia holds one of the glass slides up to the light.

Jakes Sylvia . . . what is it? What do the slides show?

Sylvia It's a fossil. Large skull . . . prominent sagittal crest . . . which means it's from the tyrannosaurid family, and that would be exciting enough except . . . (*Another slide.*) Here . . . look. Just along the edge . . . feathers.

Jai Feathers? **Theo** But what does that mean – ?

Sylvia (*gathering the slides*) I need to go to bed –

Jakes No – why don't you stay with us, Sylvia – ?

Theo Yes! Stay – please.   **Jai** Stay, Sylvia – have a drink –

Sylvia No – really – I'm sure you've all got better things to do than spending Christmas Eve with your landlady, so . . .

Clearly, they don't.

Sorry, I –

Jakes No . . . no . . . plenty to read . . .   **Theo** I'll go out . . . catch a late show or a midnight movie, maybe . . .   **Jai** No . . . no, of course . . .

The lodgers disperse. Sylvia, alone, studies the slides again.

Sylvia He did it . . . We did it . . .

Then grief and worry overwhelm . . .

Oh *Gum* . . .

20. NURSERY

Nana helps the sisters prepare for bed. Posy bounces around, ecstatic.

Posy Bun nets, tutus, leotards – *not* hand-made –

Pauline Nana, what's going on – ?

Nana Off the bed, Posy –

Posy When Gum comes home, that's everything I'm going to ask him to buy me –

Pauline Nana, why is Garnie so upset – ?

Nana Has everyone brushed their teeth – ?

Petrova How long ago did he send the parcel, Nana?

Beat.

In the letter, he called us babies. Why does he think we're still –

Nana The letter was dated 1924. 1924. He sent that parcel ten years ago –

Petrova Ten . . . Long enough for a body to turn into bone –

Nana Petrova. You know I don't like it when you talk like that –

Pauline But you haven't found any bones yet, have you? And until you find the bones –

Nana I don't think we can wait any longer. This house belongs to Gum. We can't afford to fix it, we can't afford to live in it, and we can't sell it until –

Pauline You make him legally dead.

Petrova What? *No* –

Nana (*barrelling through, practical*) But after we pay off all the debts –

Pauline Nana, what *debts* – ?

Nana There should be enough money to set us up in a small flat somewhere –

Petrova Including the lodgers?

Nana The kind of place we'll afford, love . . . it won't have room for lodgers –

Pauline I'll have to go out to work, won't I? Washing clothes, taking care of other people's children –

Nana I . . . I don't know, I –

Posy Will I still be able to take ballet lessons – ?

Petrova What about you, Nana? What happens if we don't have the money to pay you anymore – ?

Nana Petrova, I . . . I haven't been paid in five years –

Petrova You haven't been paid – ?!

Nana I'd stopped thinking about myself as someone who was *paid*, I . . . Is that . . . Is that what you all think of me – ?

| **Petrova** No . . . | **Pauline** No, of course not. | **Posy** No, you're our Nana, Nana – |

Nana No, no, into bed. You're all far too big to have me chasing you round a nursery –

Pauline Nana –

Nana Best not tell Sylvia what I . . .

Beat.

Goodnight, Fossils, I . . . Goodnight.

Nana exits.

Pauline Nice work, Petrova –

Posy You hurt her feelings, Petrova –

Petrova Gum is dead.

Pauline No . . . No, we don't know that for sure –

Posy Okay, but . . . not *really* dead . . .

Petrova He's dead. Legally dead – really dead – it doesn't matter – he isn't coming back. And without Gum . . . what are we?

Posy We're sisters –

Pauline Not really. Only by accident.

Petrova Everyone leaves. Everyone always leaves us. The lodgers will go, Nana will go, and if Garnie doesn't have enough money to keep us – nothing is tying the three of us together –

Posy There is! We all have the same last name –

Petrova (*realising*) 'Fossil'. We're all 'P. Fossil'. (*A sudden new thought.*) And I think we should try and be in as many productions as possible –

Pauline What?

Posy Petrova, you hate being on stage –

Petrova No one is going to pay a twelve-year-old to drive a car or fly an aeroplane, but they'll pay me to be a dancing playing card or the back end of a dancing caterpillar, only we need to spend the money on keeping this house, and everyone in it, together, so . . . so let's make a vow.

Pauline A vow?

Posy What's a vow?

Petrova Put your necklaces on and I'll show you –

Pauline Why do we need our –

Posy Our necklaces?

Petrova *Now.* Quickly, come on!

Necklaces on, the girls assemble in the middle of the room.

Petrova We three Fossils . . . Go on, say it . . .

Pauline We three Fossils . . .   **Posy** We three Fossils . . .

Petrova Vow to distinguish our name.

Pauline Vow to distinguish   **Posy** Vow to distinguish
our name.   our name.

Petrova So that we can make our own futures . . .

Pauline So that we can   **Posy** So that we can make our
make our own futures . . .   own futures . . .

Petrova In the absence of a past . . .

Pauline In the absence of   **Posy** In the absence of
a past . . .   a past . . .

Posy And so that we can make a lot of money –

Pauline Ugh, Posy –   **Petrova** To take care of
ourselves and everyone we
know –

Posy And five, or – or twenty –

Petrova Or a hundred million years from now –

Posy When they talk about us in the history books . . .

Petrova and Posy don't know how to finish this thought, but –

Pauline No one will say it's because of our grandfathers.

Petrova No one will say it's   **Posy** No one will say it's
because of our grandfathers.   because of our grandfathers.

Pauline raises her hand into the centre.

Pauline We vow.

Posy places her hand on Pauline's.

Posy We vow.

Petrova places hers on top.

Petrova We vow.

And just when it feels almost possible that the vow has conjured real magic . . .

Posy (*whispering*) What happens now?

Petrova Now . . . Now? . . . We *work!*

Blackout.
Interval.

Act Two

1. AN ONSTAGE REHEARSAL

A 1930s futuristic production of A Midsummer Night's Dream.
Mid-rehearsal: fairies dance through what is meant to be their enchanted woodland bower – though it scarcely resembles one.
Meanwhile, Titania, their fairy queen, is already smitten with the donkey-headed Nick Bottom.

Titania
Out of this wood do not desire to go,
Thou shalt remain here whether thou wilt or no.
I am a spirit of no common rate.
The summer still doth tend upon my state,
And I do love thee: therefore, go with me;
I'll give thee fairies to attend on thee.
Peaseblossom! Cobweb! Moth! and Mustardseed!

Pauline, Winifred, Posy and Petrova enter in costume.

Pauline (*as Peaseblossom*)
Ready!

Winifred (*as Cobweb*)
 And I.

Posy (*as Moth*)
 And I.

Petrova (*as Mustardseed*)
 And I. Where shall we go?

Mr French Stop. Petrova Fossil, say your line again, please.

Petrova 'And I. Where shall we –'

Mr French No. Listen to your sister. Pauline?

Pauline 'And I.'

Mr French Can you hear that? Can you hear what she did there? Two words. Separate. Distinct. Perfectly inflected. Try it again, please.

Petrova 'And I.'

Mr French No

Petrova 'And I.'

Mr French No.

Petrova 'And I – ?'

Mr French Petrova, what is that tucked into your costume?

Petrova It's a car brochure.

Mr French A car brochure.

Petrova I promise I'm only reading it in the breaks –

Mr French Petrova, I have a three-hour play to rehearse, only four weeks to do it in, and so far, I've spent an inordinate amount of time on the five brief moments in which you appear –

Petrova 'And I. Where shall we go?' 'Hail.' 'Mustardseed.' 'Ready.' 'What's your will?'

Underneath this, Doctor Jakes enters, concerned . . .

Mr French Is this a joke to you, Petrova – ?

Pauline She's just showing you she knows her lines, Mr French –

Mr French *I* know her lines. We all know her lines. With the right motivation a caged parrot could be taught to utter her lines –

Pauline I'll keep practising with her at home, I promise –

Mr French At this point, it would be easier to replace her –

Petrova No – !

Immediate dissent and panic erupts, then grows – rapid overlap –

Titania Walter, is that really necessary – ?

Bottom That seems a little extreme, Walter –

Posy Mr French, she can do it, I know she can do it – !

Pauline I'll practise with her every morning, every night – !

Winifred You can't replace her, Mr French – their uncle is dead, they don't have any relations, and they really *really* need the money – !

Doctor Jakes crosses the stage –

Jakes I think that's quite enough of that, don't you, Mr French?

Mr French Miss Jakes . . .

Jakes It's *Doctor* Jakes, and for what's it worth, public humiliation is unlikely to motivate professional actors, children, *or* caged parrots.

Mr French Doctor Jakes, you were hired – exclusively – as the children's chaperone –

Jakes Fortunately for you, Mr French, my skills extend beyond that, so I've jotted down a few dramaturgical notes – and do read them please. I worry, my dear, that your extraordinary imagination might be slightly overshadowing the text –

Mr French It's a futuristic production, Doctor –

Jakes But this is still *A Midsummer Night's Dream*, Mr French, and you must infuse it with *magic* –

Nana enters.

Nana Doctor Jakes, it's already past five, Mr Saran is waiting with the car – (*Re: the set.*) What monstrosity is this? (*Startled by Winifred's costume.*) Mother of – (*Turning, re: Petrova's costume*) Son of a sainted aunt! What are they supposed to be?!

Pauline We're fairies, Nana.

Nana Fairies?

Winifred Futuristic fairies.

Nana Whatever you are, it doesn't resemble any fairy I've seen –

Jakes Nana. If Mr French would like to pursue this particular interpretation of *A Midsummer Night's Dream* –

Mr French Which I do –

Jakes Then that is his prerogative as Director.

Mr French Thank you –

Jakes Give me three days, Mr French. Three. Let me borrow the costume, and Petrova, and I will return to you the fairy Mustardseed –

Mr French Each word, perfectly inflected –

Jakes Each word, perfectly inflected. Girls, you heard what Nana said, Mr Saran is waiting – Winifred, you too, dear, come along, we'll drop you home . . .

Mr French watches them go, slightly winded, but turns to face –

Nana I may not know much about much, Mr French, and certainly nothing about theatre. But I do know a thing or two about fairies *and* what they should wear. Tonight I'll have a look in my sewing box, bring you in a piece of organza. It's a crisp, sheer fabric. Wonderful for wings.

A plane flies overhead . . .

2. JUST OUTSIDE CROYDON AERODROME

Still in her costume, Petrova stands with binoculars, searching the sky. Jai leans against the car, engrossed in the Midsummer *script.*

Petrova De Havilland DH86 Express! Four engines, tapered wings, single vertical stabiliser and rudder –

Jai (*reading aloud*)
'Then, my queen, in silence sad
Trip we after night's shade . . .'

Petrova joins in, tapping the rhythm against her chest.

Petrova
'We the globe can compass soon
Swifter than the wand'ring moon.'

Jai Why is Doctor Jakes making you learn the whole scene?

Petrova So I know why people are saying what they're saying, and I don't get bored and start thinking about engines.

Jai Right. Practical.

Petrova And you can't call me Petrova –

Jai No?

Petrova My name is Mustardseed. *Captain* Mustardseed. I fight, I fly, I protect my fairy friends, and I don't have to go to any fairy balls or do any fairy dancing – *ever* – because that is my backstory and every actor is allowed to have one.

Jai smiles a little at Doctor Jakes's intervention.

Jai So . . . how long before Sylvia finds out that Peaseblossom, Moth and Captain Mustardseed are paying all the household bills?

Petrova (*lowering the binoculars*) How did you – ?

Jai produces the necklaces.

Jai Nana asked me to take these for an appraisal. Said it was your idea. Then she made me swear – by 'Christ-the-Lord-our-Saviour, O-Him-and-everything-else' – not to breathe a word of it to Sylvia.

Petrova If Garnie knows where the money came from, she won't accept it –

Jai And when she asks where the necklaces are?

Beat.

Petrova I hadn't thought that far ahead.

Jai I've given the money to Nana –

Petrova No – Jai – I would never ask you to / do that –

Jai As a loan. These necklaces are my collateral. And given the . . . well, the *highly unlikely* scenario that I'll ever need them, I promise: they'll come back in pristine condition.

Petrova We'll pay you back, Jai, I swear –

Jai I know –

Petrova Pauline, Posy and I are going for every audition we can find. Doctor Jakes says I'll never play Richard the Third, but *Jack and the Beanstalk*'s coming up, and Theo says there's every chance I'll be cast as a dancing bean!

Jai Speaking of dancing –

Petrova Don't. Please. This is the only day I have free from it –

Jai It's also the only day I have with you. And I need some help. I was wondering . . . in exchange for the driving lessons, the necklace keeping, and the, uh . . . the trips to Croydon Aerodrome . . . I was wondering . . . if you might, uh . . . teach me?

Petrova You want to learn ballet?

Jai Not ballet, just . . . something modern . . . maybe? Something that might be useful for . . . I don't know . . . if you want to take a lady out for dinner –

Petrova Who – ?

Jai No one. No one in particular, but . . . someone, someday –

Petrova If you're trying to find a wife, Jai, just make sure she doesn't have any children. You've only got the one room and we're not getting rid of any more fossils –

Jai Petrova, I have to move anyway. Your family is selling the house –

Petrova No one's bought it yet –

Jai Yes, but I don't intend to stay in a single room forever.

Petrova So you're planning on leaving?

Jai Well not right now, but . . .

Petrova After you meet a woman. And take her dancing.

Jai Well, I doubt it's going to be as easy as 'woman, waltz, and happily ever after', but –

Petrova Right, then we better get started.

Petrova turns on the radio.

The first dance I'm going to teach you . . . begins in a tall commanding position . . . arms bent at the elbows –

Jai Petrova . . . no ballet, right?

Petrova Don't worry, Jai. At the Children's Academy, they teach you all the latest dance crazes. Including this one. Arms bent, please. And fingers curled. Like *claws* . . .

3. MADAME FIDOLIA'S OFFICE, THE CHILDREN'S ACADEMY

Madame Fidolia reads a letter to Posy.

Fidolia 'Dear Miss Fidolia. Thank you for your letter of recommendation. We would be pleased to see your student, Posy Fossil, for an audition this autumn.'

Pause.

The Vic-Wells Ballet School. It's no Imperial Ballet, but in this land of Marmite and crumpets, it's the best I could do.

Posy, confused.

This is good news, Posy –

Posy You . . . You don't want to teach me anymore – ?

Fidolia I cannot. You need dedicated training. I have a Children's Stage Academy to run. Teapots for *Alice*. Fairies for *Midsummer*. This morning, a troupe of tap-dancing oysters rehearsing upstairs – right now, I need to find twelve dancing puddings for *A Christmas Carol* – I hate it. Passionately. But this past year I've felt something close to genuine love returning –

Posy Why – ?

Fidolia Because now I'm teaching you. And what I see for you, my Posy, is much more than Fairy Number Three in some ridiculous production. So. You feign ignorance if that Mr French asks you to perform anything difficult. You have an audition in three months. I won't have you injuring yourself –

Posy Madame?

Fidolia Yes, my Posy?

Posy Will it cost money? To go to this school?

Fidolia Ballet *always* costs money –

Posy Then I can't go. Even if I wanted to. When things cost money, Garnie always says no, and – and I made a vow –

Fidolia A vow – ?

Posy I need to make money for my family – not *spend* it –

Fidolia You haven't been accepted yet. But if you are, my Posy . . . don't worry . . . I will help you speak to them.

Beat.

Posy Madame?

Fidolia Yes, Posy?

Posy Did you throw away my shoes?

Fidolia Of course not.

Posy Can I have them back?

Fidolia (*already leaving*) I will think about it –

Posy But Madame –

Fidolia Puddings, Posy. I have twelve dancing puddings to find.

4. FLYING REHEARSAL

Above, Titania is 'flown', but struggles with her fear of heights.

Titania
  First, rehearse your song by rote
  To each word a warbling note:
  Hand in hand, with fairy grace,
  Will we . . . sing, and . . . oh God . . . bless this place.

Then Oberon rises. He finds himself, inexplicably, upside down, and then, struggling to right himself, remains there.

Oberon
  Now, until the break of day,
  Through this house each fairy stray –

Mr French Stop! Stop! Is there any way to keep Oberon the right way up, please –

Fly Operator I've already told him, he'll stay upright if he engages his core –

Oberon (*still upside down*) I'm an actor, sweetheart, not an athlete, and all of my training, thus far, has been exclusively on the ground –

Titania Walter, please, can I come down . . . please . . .

Mr French Bring them down! One week of extra flight training, specialised crew, a custom-made apparatus, and this . . . this is what we manage –

Petrova Can I try?

Pauline (*quiet*) Petrova, don't.

Mr French Who said that? Who? Go on, speak up!

Petrova Me!

Pauline *Petrova* –

Mr French You?! Oh no, no, little friend, we've lost enough time on you already –

Petrova I've been taking ballet lessons almost every day for over a year. I can hold any position you want me to – I could probably dance up there if you needed it –

Mr French And what about your lines? How would they sound? From up there –

Petrova Clip me up and we'll find out –

> *She steps into the harness, ready to be clipped. Mr French shrugs, motions to the Fly Operator to secure her.*

Stage Manager Mr French, just to flag – there might be a few child-labour laws to consider first –

Mr French Do you have a fear of heights, Petrova?

Petrova I don't know –

Mr French Wonderful.

Fly Operator This is just a little test lift – okay, Petrova?

Petrova Okay . . .

> *She's raised a little way off the ground.*

Fly Operator How does that feel?

Petrova Um . . . can I go any higher – ?

Fly Operator (*shouting*) Let's take her all the way up . . .

> *Petrova rises up above the stage. Gasps and murmurs from the cast.*

Mr French Miss Fossil, indulge me, is there any way you could deliver your opening line from up there?

Petrova 'And I.'

Mr French (*surprised*) What? What was that?

Petrova 'And I.'

Mr French Again.

Petrova 'And I.'

Mr French (*motioning to the crew to bring her down*) Petrova . . . I've just had an idea –

Stage Manager Oh – wonderful –

Mr French Do you think you could possibly say it while moving –

Petrova I can try – !

Stage Manager Oh – God –

Petrova (*soaring, ecstatic*) 'And I', 'And I', 'And I And I And I And I!' 'Where shall we go!'

Mr French (*thrilled*) Now all of your lines, you magical fairy creature – !

Petrova 'Hail!' 'Mustardseed!' 'Ready!' 'What is your will!'

Petrova, in glorious flight . . .
   But just as Petrova reaches some sort of zenith, the sky itself begins to crumble –

5. HOME

. . . a section of the ceiling has given away. Sky light pierces through, carrying with it a cascade of dust and debris.
   Petrova descends.
   Sylvia, Nana, Pauline and Posy stare up at the newly formed hole.
   Doctor Jakes and Theo, alarmed, emerge from their rooms, to join them.

Theo What in the –

Jakes Dear God, you can see all the way through –

Sylvia Water damage. Probably a few broken roof slates.

Jakes I did try to warn you, Sylvia, 'a leaky roof left unchecked –'

Sylvia It was on the list, Doctor. But so was fixing the boiler, clearing the chimneys, updating the wiring, and fighting the mould just . . . just everywhere –

She starts to cry, stifles it, heads towards a cupboard. At the same time, Jai, his nerve bolstered, enters with flowers.

Jai Excuse me, Sylvia, I – (*Realising everyone else is there.*) Hello . . . everyone – (*Seeing the roof.*) Oh my God –

Sylvia I'm just . . . I'm just going to sit in here for a while.

Jakes Sweetheart, that's the linen cupboard –

Sylvia (*from inside*) I'm aware! Thank you, Doctor Jakes!

Jai I'll call some people, see if I can find a roofer –

Theo I'll call around too. I know a few people who might be able to help –

Jakes And who would that be, Miss Dane – a chorus of tiny tap-dancing children –

Theo Set builders, actually. But if you'd like them to dance for you, Doctor, I'm sure I can arrange that too . . .

Nana Come with me, Doctor. Let's see if we can find a bigger bucket. Pauline, make sure your sisters stay away from the hole!

Once alone . . .

Petrova How much of our *Midsummer* money is left?

Pauline It's gone. Nana needed to fix the stove before Garnie found out it was broken, you and I needed new ballet shoes, Posy is going through three pairs a week –

Petrova Can't you ask Mr French for more work?

Pauline I have. None of his next three productions use children –

Petrova But we need another play, Pauline, you can't give up now –

Pauline And what exactly are you doing to help – ?

Petrova I made the vow – !

Pauline The vow isn't real, Petrova, the vow is stupid –

Petrova The vow is not stupid, it's a solemn unbreakable promise –

Pauline To who – ?!

Petrova To ourselves! To – to the universe! To – to *God* – !

Pauline Well, no one is listening – !!

Posy dives in.

Posy We three Fossils vow to make history because we don't have any history but we do have a name and if we put that name into history we'll earn lots of money and we'll be really famous and we'll fix the roof and no one will say it's because of our grandfathers.

Posy thrusts her hand into the centre.

We vow.

Petrova places her hand on Posy's. Glares at Pauline.

Petrova We vow.

Pauline, gritting her teeth, places her hand on top.

Pauline We vow.

Petrova adds a flourish:

Petrova Amen.

Immediately, the phone rings. The children stare at it.

Pauline (*calling out*) I'll get it. (*Answering.*) Hello, this is Pauline Fossil speaking . . .

As the house gives way, Petrova and Posy stare at their hands, at each other, and then up to the sky . . . marvelling at their capacity to invoke a higher power . . .

6. A FILM STUDIO

Pauline enters an expansive indoor film studio, with large cameras mounted on wheeled dollies for movement, a bustling hub of activity and 1930s glamour.

Pauline is dressed and heavily made-up as 'Princess Henrietta', a 1650s English princess exiled to the French court.

The director, Mr Sholsky, enters.

Mr Sholsky Miss Fossil, you've learnt your lines, I hope –

Pauline I think so – ?

Mr Sholsky Good –

Pauline But I only received a few pages. I was hoping to maybe read the full script – ?

Mr Sholsky No need. Your scene partner, Arthur –

Arthur (*at the buffet table*) Hi –

Mr Sholsky Veteran, sixteenth film, just let him do the work, and respond with your lines – Arthur, ready?

Arthur (*mouth full*) Yep.

Mr Sholsky (*shouting out*) Clear the set please . . . Silence . . .

Pauline watches as the unassuming Arthur quickly downs his lunch.

Clapper *Charles the Exile.* Scene Eighty-Four. Take One.

Mr Sholsky Action.

Arthur transforms.

Arthur (*as Charles*) Write to me, Henrietta, while I am gone.

Pauline (*as Henrietta*) I will try.

Arthur (*as Charles*) Not 'I will try'. Say, 'I will.'

Pauline (*as Henrietta*) I will. I will.

Mr Sholsky Cut. I will . . . what? 'I will happily', 'I will unreservedly' – What are you trying to say, Miss Fossil – ?

Pauline I don't know –

Mr Sholsky This is your brother. Charles the Second. Right now you're both in exile, hiding out in the fancy French court, but Charles here has decided to waltz back to England, stake his claim on the English throne. Problem is, last time you were both there, they beheaded your father, / Charles the First –

Pauline Charles the First – I know – Doctor Jakes and I read every history book we could find –

Mr Sholsky Good, let's go again –

Pauline Except I don't know which part of the story this scene is in –

Mr Sholsky I don't need you to tell a whole story, Miss Fossil, I need you to summon a feeling, and quickly – Arthur, Scene Eighty-Two, show her –

Arthur snaps in.

Arthur (*as Charles*) Mother, I understand the shadows that my father's fate casts upon this family. But hiding here, in the lavish corridors of this French chateau, only deepens the shadows. I cannot remain in exile forever; I *must* go back to England.

Arthur snaps out.

Mr Sholsky There. See, Pauline? *That* is performing for film –

Pauline It was extraordinary –

Arthur Thank you –

Pauline Can I just ask a question, please – ?

Mr Sholsky One question – quickly.

Pauline Why go back?

Mr Sholsky Why . . . go back – ?

Pauline They killed our father; they could kill my brother too –

Mr Sholsky Haven't you ever wanted something, Miss Fossil?

Pauline I want to be an actress, but I probably wouldn't die for it –

Mr Sholsky Good. Use that point of difference. Look at your brother, silly little boy-prince going off on his dangerous little quest –

Pauline Exactly –

Mr Sholsky But this brother of yours, he's not like you, is he? He's singular in his focus – relentless. And while his ambitions might baffle or even exasperate you, it doesn't matter –

Pauline He's my brother.

As Mr Sholsky talks, Pauline looks past him and notices Posy and Petrova have entered – perhaps tussling for the best view but watching on, and proudly.

Mr Sholsky You played together, grieved together, survived together – your past is his past – every moment, irrevocably intertwined – and now, as he stands at the threshold of his own separate journey, the realisation hits: these simple words, 'I will,' could be your final exchange – (*Catching a fleeting emotion in Pauline.*) Arthur, food down – everyone, silence on set!

Clapper *Charles the Exile*. Scene Eighty-Four. Take Two.

Mr Sholsky Action.

Arthur (*as Charles*) Write to me, Henrietta, while I am gone.

Pauline (*as Henrietta*) I will try.

Arthur (*as Charles*) Not 'I will try'. Say, 'I will.'

Pauline (*as Henrietta*) I will. I will.

Pauline delivers. As 'Charles' departs, the camera captures 'Henrietta' in tight close-up.

Mr Sholsky Cut. Well done, Pauline, moving on!

Pauline attempts to shake off her character, but she's visibly unsettled, mind racing with thoughts of her sisters . . .

7. THE CHILDREN'S ACADEMY

Posy, alone practising . . .
Madame Fidolia enters.

Fidolia Posy, what are you still doing here?

Posy It's not perfect yet –

Fidolia It's not. But the examiners won't expect perfection. If they did, then this new school would have nothing to teach you.

Posy Madame . . . what if I don't get in?

Fidolia Then we find another way –

Posy What if I'm not good enough? What if I didn't work hard enough – ?

Fidolia You have –

Posy Maybe I didn't give enough –

Fidolia Posy –

Posy My mother gave up everything. *Everything*. My mother gave up *me*.

Fidolia Are you angry with her? For doing that?

Posy No. I'd do the same. I'd give up anything –

Fidolia Oh . . . Posy.

Pause, Fidolia softens.

I have known so many dancers. They build their whole selves out of satin and rosin. And when they fall – and they *always* fall – that's when they discover . . . they have no idea how to rise. And why? Because resilience . . . *true* resilience . . . That comes from knowing everything else that you are –

Posy But . . . what if ballet really is the only thing that you know about yourself – ?

Fidolia You are a sister. A daughter. A rascal. My daily headache. Perhaps . . . one day . . . a mother. Take it from a wrinkled old bat: you make yourself one thing only, you make yourself far too easily broken.

Beat.

Also, when you finish your audition, remember to complete your révérence –

Posy But it's not a class –

Fidolia It is the way to say thank you. To the examiners. To the pianist. And one day, when you are standing on a grand stage . . . there you will thank your partner for dancing with you . . . you will thank the conductor for their beautiful music . . . and most important of all . . . you will thank the audience . . . for the honour of their time.

Posy One day . . . when I know you're in the audience, Madame . . . then my révérence will be for you –

Fidolia *Chepuka* [nonsense], Posy. You won't even remember me –

Posy I will –

Fidolia Go home. Rest. I'll see you back here at eight o'clock tomorrow morning – and don't be late. The examiners will forgive your lack of technique, they won't abide a lack of punctuality.

Posy I'll remember you always, Madame . . . (*Cheekily.*) Federovsky . . .

Posy grins, and runs off before Madame Fidolia has a chance to admonish her.
Alarmed, Madame Fidolia glances around, to see if anyone has heard, but catches her own reflection in the mirror.
Madame Fidolia begins a familiar ballet sequence. But pain and breathlessness soon overwhelm her.
Behind her, Katerina enters. Madame Fidolia watches as another figure joins her . . . Nikki . . . in all the finery of a Russian Prince . . . and so the second chapter of Katerina's story unfolds . . .
Briefly, Katerina surrenders to the romance, but chaos erupts – revolution strikes.
Nikki vanishes. Katerina finds her life suddenly at risk.
In her extravagant home, Katerina packs what she can, filling her pockets and suitcase with jewellery and finery. Faced with an over-abundance of sentimental items, she opts for the framed portrait only.
An arduous journey follows, with rich and poor refugees alike, across Russia, onto an overcrowded boat, then through Europe. Throughout, Katerina's health deteriorates.
Finally, she reaches London, where she faces not just poverty, but also obscurity. Katerina tries to dance again, but her failing health betrays her.
To survive, she sells the last of her possessions, and turns to teaching. But the shame of her reduced circumstances compels her to hide both her portrait and her true identity. Katerina transforms into Madame Fidolia, complete with her wooden cane.

> *Night turns to morning, and Katerina departs, or fades, or perhaps dances on forever . . . leaving only Madame Fidolia behind.*
> *Posy re-enters, now dressed in her audition attire.*

Posy I'm ready, Madame.

> *But Madame Fidolia doesn't respond.*

Madame?

> *Posy realises –*

Madame –

8. HOME

Mid-argument . . .

Sylvia No, Pauline – absolutely not –

Pauline But Garnie –

Sylvia You're fifteen. I'm not sending you off – all alone – halfway across the world –

Petrova (*newly alarmed*) Halfway across the world?

Sylvia *California*, Pauline –

Pauline But this is what I want, Garnie! I *want* to be an actor – !

Sylvia Do you understand what the studio wants in return?

Jakes (*reviewing the contract*) Five pictures –

Pauline Five pictures!

Jakes Three years –

Sylvia Three years!

Jakes Gruelling hours, no schooling –

Nana Excuse me?! **Pauline** It might not be like that all!

Jakes What happened to RADA? I thought you wanted to finish your education, then train as a theatre actress –

Pauline Money! Money happened! More than we've ever seen! Enough to take care of ourselves and everyone we know –

Sylvia If you sign this, Pauline, it's your money. Not ours.

Pauline No, it's for us – all of us –

Sylvia We don't need your money Pauline –

Pauline I'm not a kid anymore, Garnie – we're poor, you don't need to hide it from me –

Sylvia We're not poor, you are still a child, and part of the privilege of being a child is that you don't have to concern yourself with the state of your family's finances –

Pauline Nana, Petrova, Posy and I – we discuss it all the time! The only reason we had all the school materials we needed this year is because *Midsummer* paid for it –

Sylvia (to *Nana*) No – no, you said the school was getting rid of a surplus –

Pauline And the only reason we have a literal roof over our heads is because of *Charles the Exile* –

Sylvia Jai found the roofers, you negotiated the rate –

Jai I'm a good negotiator, Sylvia. I'm not that good.

Sylvia So you've all . . . what? You've all been lying to me – ?

Nana The girls wanted to help you –

Sylvia I want them to be children! *Children!* When they came into this house, I made each of them a promise: you are here now, you are safe, but you won't just survive, you will *thrive* and –

Pauline But if I sign this contract, then we can all keep the house –

Sylvia *Damn* the house!

Petrova Garnie . . . it belonged to Gum –

Sylvia Damn him too! Stupid *stupid* man, leaving us, years at a time, getting himself killed in the process – no, no – I'm grateful to him, I am, for giving me a home – for giving all of us a home – but now I would like to leave this home before I *hate* this home because I don't want to spend money on a *house,* I want to spend it on all of you –

Petrova What about the lodgers? It's their home too, where are they going to live – ?

Sylvia Petrova, I love our lodgers just as much as you do, but Theo, Jai, Doctor Jakes – they are not my responsibility –

Petrova Why not – ?

Sylvia Because they pay to be here – !

Petrova SO DO WE!

As Sylvia reels, winded, Posy bursts through the front door, Theo in pursuit.

Theo Posy . . . Posy . . . Posy, wait, *please* –

Nana Posy Fossil, you stop right now.

Posy stops. Turns. She's visibly upset.

Nana Theo . . . what's going on?

Theo Posy . . . Posy was very brave today –

Posy Just say it. Madame is dead. We called an ambulance – they told us to call a funeral house instead – and then we had to wait for the undertakers for almost four hours –

Sylvia Poor Madame –

Posy Poor Madame?! What about me?! I had an audition today. To the only full-time ballet school in the country. And

Madame was supposed to take me, and I didn't tell you, because if I got in, it was going to cost money, and when things cost money, you say no, but it doesn't matter because I missed the audition, and Madame is dead, and now there's no one to train me except Theo, and she's not a good enough dancer –

Sylvia Posy Fossil – **Theo** (*to Sylvia*) Don't –

Posy She's not! You might think she's a good dancer, but that's because you know *nothing* about ballet –

Sylvia That is enough! It's all very well to be ambitious, Posy, but if ambition is going to kill everything nice about you, perhaps we need to rethink this ballet business altogether –

Posy Why did you even take me in?! Why didn't you send me somewhere else? To someone who understands me? Ballet dancers don't get to be ballet dancers forever, they have to start when they're young, at the age I am now, and this was my once-in-a-lifetime chance –

Sylvia Posy, today a woman died –

Posy I know! I found her!

Posy runs off, up into the nursery.
We follow her . . .

9. NURSERY

Posy packs a runaway bag in a fit of grief-stricken rage. She turns to retrieve her mother's ballet shoes from the wall – a pang of regret: she gave them to Madame. For a moment, this throws her, but Posy grits her teeth, moves to the window, ready to make her escape.
Pauline and Petrova appear in the doorway.

Petrova I wouldn't. That's how I broke my leg. Four years ago. After a fight with Pauline.

Pauline The kitchen door is probably safest.

Petrova But you need to wait until everyone's gone to bed.

Pauline By which time, maybe, you'll have calmed down enough to talk to us?

Theo enters.

Theo Or me? Perhaps?

She extends a carefully wrapped package.

This was in Madame's office. Your name is on it. I wanted to give it to you at the Academy, but you left so quickly . . .

Posy (*reads the note*) 'To my Posy. Confidence . . . and humility.'

Tearing off the wrapping, Posy is met with her mother's shoes, either wrapped in their own ribbons or carefully showcased and preserved in a glass box.
Silence.

Theo . . . I'm sorry if what I said hurt your feelings –

Theo You were right, Posy.

Posy . . . I was?

Theo I'm not good enough to be your teacher. Sylvia, Nana – they won't understand that. But I do. Because I love dance. Just as much as you do. I've built an entire career off the back of it – so I also know just how often it tells a person they don't belong.

But the thing is, Posy . . . human beings have danced as long as they've existed. And Miss Theo Dane? That is the greatest role I've ever had. Because now I'm able to remind my students that dance is for everyone, and also . . . dance is something *to enjoy*.

So. While I try to find someone else to take you for lessons, why don't you and I just . . . enjoy it? Together?

Posy Okay.

Theo There's a *Coppélia* in town. And a *Swan Lake*. Tomorrow night, The Manoff Ballet is premiering a new piece –

Posy The Manoff Ballet? Juliette Manoff? Juliette Manoff is in London – ?

Theo You've heard of her – ?

Posy I need to see her –

Theo She doesn't perform anymore, Posy, she choreographs –

As she speaks, Posy removes the shoes she's wearing, and either untangles the ribbons or breaks open the glass box to try on her mother's shoes.

Posy Juliette Manoff gave the greatest performance Madame had ever seen. And if I can't go to ballet school in London, then I want to learn from Manoff, and right now, Manoff is in London –

Theo Yes, but . . . Posy, her school is in Paris – !

Posy (*the shoes*) They fit.

A moment. Brief. Then Posy whips off the ballet shoes, and begins expertly breaking them in.

I'm going to find Manoff. I'm going to ask her to teach me, and if you want to help me, then help me find her – *please* – but if you're not going to help me, then –

Pauline Do you know where Manoff is rehearsing, Theo?

Theo I . . . I do, but –

Pauline Will you take us to her – ?

Posy Tonight – it needs to be tonight –

Pauline If Manoff is as good as Madame said she is –

Posy She's the best. You understand that . . . don't you, Theo?

Theo looks between Posy and Pauline, both resolute. Petrova, sensing her world is about to crumble, stands apart.

Theo Right. Okay –

Pauline Okay – ?

Theo Yes. Okay. Okay! *Let's do this!*

Posy *Let's do this – !*

Theo But before we do this, uh . . . I just need to see how much money I have to get us all onto a bus, or into a taxicab –

Petrova You don't need to worry about money, Theo. I have a better idea.

10. BATHROOM

Nana, outside a closed bathroom door. The sound of running water.

Nana Sylvia . . . Sylvia, I'm coming in –

Sylvia I'm just taking a bath, Nana – !

Nana (*entering*) If you were having a real bath, you'd have flooded the house by now –

Sylvia is in the empty bathtub. She's been crying. Nana turns off the tap.

Sylvia Borrowed that trick from Pauline. I was spending too much time in the linen cupboard. Thought I'd shake it up a bit.

Nana Any room in there for me?

Sylvia moves aside. Nana climbs into the bathtub.

Sylvia Am I doing a terrible job of raising them?

Nana No.

Sylvia But I don't know what I am to them. I'm too old to be their sister, I'm too young to be their mother –

Nana You're Garnie. You're their guardian.

Sylvia And it's my responsibility to take care of them.

Nana And it's my responsibility to take care of you.

Sylvia No – Nana, I'm not a child –

Nana You can do all the growing you like, Sylvia . . . I'll still see the little girl who arrived with a letter, and a suitcase, and then filled this house with her messy pots of paint . . .

Sylvia nestles in, allows herself to be comforted.
Jai enters.

Jai Oh – sorry . . . sorry . . . The door, it . . . it wasn't locked –

Sylvia I, uh . . . I forgot to put the lock back after Pauline shut herself in –

Jai I didn't mean to disturb –

Nana Good of you to join us, Mr Saran. Sylvia here was just saying how much she'd like to leave the house for a bit –

Jai Really – ?

Sylvia No – Nana –

Nana I, of course, need to stay and look after the children . . .

Nana slips away.

Sylvia Jai, you really don't have to –

Jai Dinner, maybe? Some dancing?

Sylvia Oh . . . oh, Jai –

Jai Oh dear –

Sylvia I'm sorry if I gave you the wrong impression –

Jai It's fine, honestly, I –

Sylvia Just because I'm raising three budding ballerinas doesn't mean I'm one of them.

Beat.

I'm a really *really* bad dancer, Jai . . .

Jai begins doing . . . something.

Sylvia What is that? What are you doing?

Jai Petrova taught me. She calls this one the 'Tyranno-Temptation-Tango'. Instead of grasping a woman in a passionate embrace, I'm supposed to maintain a distance of approximately two to three feet, tuck my elbows in, make myself some little claw hands, and then I sort of . . . strut around the dance floor, and every so often let out an exaggerated roar . . . *Roar!*

Sylvia And that's . . . supposed to attract a lady, is it?

Jai It was at this point I realised that Petrova Fossil may not actually be interested in improving my chances of romance . . .

Sylvia I think Petrova Fossil might be underestimating the power of those little claw hands . . .

Jai draws her close, initiating a tender, slow dance, and then remembers –

Jai Sorry, I just . . .

Sylvia What?

Jai I did really need to use the bathroom –

Sylvia Go –

Jai I won't be long – I – I don't know why I'm telling you how long I'm going to be –

Sylvia Go! (*Realising she's the one who needs to leave.*) I'll go!

In the hallway, Sylvia continues dancing – something unencumbered, joy-filled – like how small children dance before they grow up and start caring what others think.

Jai re-enters. Watches her. Then follows suit.
As they move through the house, Sylvia and Jai collect coats, hats, gloves, everything they need for a night out. They're on the cusp of departing when . . .

Sylvia Wait. It's quiet. Too quiet.

Jakes (*entering*) Sylvia, the children are gone –

Sylvia What – ?!

Jakes I found a letter on the kitchen table –

Sylvia (*reading*) 'Dear Garnie. We've taken Posy to audition for Juliette Manoff of the Manoff Ballet. I know you will be angry with us, what with Posy in disgrace, and Petrova borrowing the car . . .'

Jai Uh . . . where's my car?

Sylvia '. . . but Petrova says to reassure you that Mr Saran is an excellent teacher, and even though she's never driven on a main road, or, indeed, at night, she promises she knows, instinctually, what she's doing.' (*Furious, to Jai.*) You taught a thirteen-year-old how to drive – ?!

11. A LONDON ROAD

Pauline 'P.S. If you're feeling at all alarmed by this letter, please be doubly reassured that Theo is with us and therefore we are being supervised by an adult at all times . . .'

Petrova, driving, open top; everyone else shouting over the road noise.

Theo (*terrified*) No no no no no no *no* – !

Posy Step on it, Petrova, can't you go any faster – ?!

Theo I believe this is already plenty fast, Posy –

Pauline (*with a map*) Stay on Cromwell Road, Petrova, then turn right onto Beauchamp Place –

Posy Wouldn't driving right through the middle of Hyde Park be faster – ?

Pauline No, she needs to turn onto Beauchamp –

Posy Give me the map, Pauline –

Pauline Get out of my seat, Posy –

Posy You don't know where you're going –

Theo No – no – this is not the day I'm going to die! I did not reinvent myself ten times over to end my life as the woman who died because *a child* was driving the car – !

Petrova brings the car to a decisive stop.

Petrova Right. Listen. All of you. I am the driver so I need to concentrate. And I can't concentrate if people are fighting or moving around in their seats – it makes this deeply unsafe for all of us. Pauline is the navigator, and she is the only one who should be talking. Is that understood?

Theo Yes. Understood.

Posy Thank you, Petrova.

Pauline Aye-aye, Captain Mustardseed.

12. BACK AT HOME

Sylvia (*on the phone*) Yes, hello – I need a taxi immediately, Nine Hundred and Ninety-Nine, Cromwell Road – last house – very long street – thank you – and please hurry.

Jai Sylvia, wait –

Sylvia I can't speak to you right now, Jai –

Jai I promise you, she's a really good driver –

Sylvia *Thirteen,* Jai! Thirteen!

They exit, still arguing. Nana quietly picks up the phone again, dials a number.

Nana (*affecting Sylvia's voice*) Hello there. Yes, I just called about a taxi – that's right – last house – very long street. We won't need a taxi immediately, so if you wouldn't mind waiting fifteen minutes or so before despatching one, that should be enough. Thank you very much.

Doctor Jakes, watching as Nana replaces the receiver.

Nana I wanted to give them a head start.

Jakes You continue to surprise me, Nana . . .

Nana (*gathering her things*) Over the course of my life, Doctor, I've had to reconcile my faith with the existence of dinosaurs, fairies and lesbians. A bit of heavily supervised underage driving is hardly going to faze me.

Beat.

Are you coming?

Jakes Me? No . . . no, I suspect this one is a family matter –

Nana Are you coming, Doctor?

Beat. Doctor Jakes follows Nana out the front door . . .

13. ON A WEST END STAGE

A Professional Ballet Dancer moves across the stage in rehearsal.
Posy wanders in. Watches the dancer at work.
An old question lingers for Posy . . . Could this be her mother? But also a new question . . . Could this be her future? Both possibilities are suspended.
Juliette Manoff enters – interrupts –

Manoff This isn't a public rehearsal, child . . . Are you lost?

Posy I'm here to see Juliette Manoff.

Manoff I'm afraid Juliette Manoff is busy.

Posy (*the dancer*) Is that –

Manoff Juliette Manoff is sixty-six years old. Does that woman look sixty-six?

Posy You're her, aren't you?

Manoff I don't need the interruption, child. I have a show opening tomorrow night and a new lead to rehearse –

Posy I missed my audition today. For the Vic-Wells Ballet School. I'm already eleven, I won't have another chance.

Manoff Why bring this disappointment to me?

Posy For a brief moment, my teacher was the greatest ballet dancer in the world, and she told me that you were even better than her –

Manoff And what is your teacher's name?

Posy Madame Fidolia.

Manoff Oh, Madame Fidolia, is it?

Posy Yes –

Manoff Another faux-Russian name peddled to stupid British children eager to learn ballet – 'Fidolia'? Really – ?

Posy What about Katerina Fedorovsky?

Beat.

Manoff I assumed she died. A very long time ago –

Posy She died this morning. In her stage training school in West London.

Manoff Who are you?

Posy Posy. Posy Fossil –

A commotion from outside. A Stage-Door Keeper enters with:

Stage-Door Keeper Right this way, ladies –

Theo *Dégagez* your hands, Monsieur! / *Dé-ga-gez* – !

Pauline *Je suis une ballerine, Monsieur!* / *Je suis une ballerine française* – !

Petrova Piqué passé! Piqué passé! Plié, tombé, pas de bourrée – !

Stage-Door Keeper I'm sorry to interrupt, Miss Manoff, but I found these three lurking in the foyer, pretending to be French –

Theo Madame Manoff, if we could have a moment of your time –

Manoff Excuse me, but you cannot just –

Pauline Enough chatter, Posy, show the woman –

Theo Oh . . . dear . . .   **Stage-Door Keeper** Don't worry, Miss Manoff, I'm on it –

Pauline I'll take the stage-door keeper, Petrova – you tackle the ballerina – !

Petrova Got it!

Theo (*warning*) Girls – wait – oh God – I'm so sorry, Madame Manoff –

Underneath the chaos, Posy begins her audition dance. It's distracted, shaky – and with the cacophony behind her . . . no one is watching.
    Then – she falls.
    Now, and for the wrong reason, Posy has the full attention of the room.
    Posy stays down for a moment. Embarrassed. Upset. Pauline moves to help.

Pauline Posy . . .

But before she can reach her . . .

Posy Don't. I'm okay.

Posy rises.
She begins again. From the top.
The music swells alongside her.
This dance builds on the various training sequences we've seen before, a radical application of each 'boring' ballet exercise. And beneath it all lies Posy's grief, anger and bitter disappointment. But at a certain point, even this is released, and Posy, while dancing, seems both wholly alive and utterly transfixed.
Sylvia, Jai, Doctor Jakes and Nana enter.
Unaware, Posy continues her dance.
Sylvia moves to interrupt, but Nana gently stays her hand.
Sylvia watches Posy, for the first time understanding that this child possesses an incredible gift.
When she finishes, Posy offers a heartfelt révérence to her teacher, Madame Fidolia, almost forgetting that anyone else is there, until –

Manoff There's a fine line between confidence and impertinence, child. Which are you?

Sylvia Confident. She's confident. Confident enough to ask for what she needs. And what she needs is to learn. From you.

Posy turns and rushes back to Sylvia. She takes her hand.
The rest of the family gather behind them.
Together, they stare Manoff down.

Manoff You understand . . . my school is in Paris.

Sylvia We'll find a way to make it work –

Manoff Even then, the child has six years of training ahead of her. That is six years of expenses to pay for –

Pauline I'll pay for it. I'll pay for everything –

Sylvia Pauline – no –

Pauline I'll sign the contract, I'll move to America –

Sylvia It's not your responsibility –

Pauline Yes, it is. You've done enough, Garnie. And this is my family too. Let me help. Please.

Manoff So, we have a decision?

Everyone defers to Sylvia.
Sylvia nods.
Posy launches herself at Sylvia – a big hug.

Posy Thank you, Garnie. *Thank you.*

And then the same to Pauline.

Thank you . . . *thank you.*

With mixed feelings, Petrova steps away from the scene . . .

14. TRANSITION – THE FOSSIL HOME

The house empties of items – sold, disposed of, or packed into luggage cases.
  Petrova does her best to retain a few items – fossils, mementos, etc.
  Sylvia, seeing her distress, offers a solution . . .

15. BACK GARDEN

. . . a home-made time capsule, near a freshly excavated pit in the back garden.
  Pauline, Petrova and Posy fill the capsule.
  The rest of the household gather to watch.

Pauline Words. For the stage. Some old. Some modern. None meant to be read exclusively in your mind.

Posy A pair of ballet shoes. Tried on a thousand times. Worn . . . once.

Petrova A model aeroplane. A car magazine. A carabiner clip from a stage-flying harness. A monkey wrench, a spark-plug spanner, a pair of grease-covered overalls.

Sylvia There. Those items should survive the next two to three hundred years . . . at least! What a *thrill* for the person who uncovers them . . .

From inside the house – a voice –

Voice (*off*) Why is no one answering the front door? Where is everyone? Where are all my things?! There used to be hundreds and hundreds of fossils just . . . just everywhere and . . .

A man emerges out into the garden.
Sylvia gasps, then turns – deep shock.
It's Gum. He's older, travel-ravaged, shabbily dressed – wooden leg – somehow smaller and more vulnerable when he isn't shrouded in imagination or memory.
Gum studies the group, confused . . . and a little frightened.

Gum I'm sorry, I . . . I thought I used to live here . . . I had a fall, you see . . . altitude sickness . . . hypothermia . . . fair bit of memory loss, a prolonged period dazed and confused in a remote Patagonian hospital – anyway, it's not important. I must have the wrong house, I . . . I'll try the next one –

Petrova Is it possible, sir . . . Is it possible that you are . . . Gum?

Gum Gum? No . . . no, gum is a viscous substance extracted from trees, or possibly short for chewing gum or bubble-gum or gumboot or gumdrop – it is not, I'm afraid, the name of an adult British male –

Petrova It's an acronym. G-U-M. Great-Uncle / Matthew . . .

Gum (*remembering*) Matthew. Great . . . Uncle . . . Matthew . . .

Beat.

Who are you?

Petrova Petrova.

Gum Petrova . . . no . . . Petrova can't be more than five years old –

Pauline I'm Pauline –

Gum You can't be –

Posy I'm Posy –

Gum Posy? But Posy's a baby –

Nana Babies grow up, Professor.

Gum Miss Gutheridge, I . . . Yes . . . Yes, I suppose they do. (*Sudden fear.*) Where is Sylvia? Sylvia . . . Where is my Sylvia?

Sylvia emerges.

Sylvia . . . my darling . . . you're not going to believe what happened to me, but –

Sylvia slaps him. Then hugs him. Hard.

I've been away a long time, haven't I?

Sylvia *Eleven years.*

Gum Eleven years. Long enough to turn into bone . . .

Nana We had to sell the house, Gum –

Petrova But I tried to keep as many of your fossils as possible –

Gum It's all right, Petrova –

Pauline We're leaving, Gum –

Gum Leaving – ?

Pauline I'm going to California with Doctor Jakes to be an actress –

Gum An actress? Doctor Jakes – ?

Jakes Hello, Professor –

Posy I'm going to Paris with Nana to study ballet –

Gum Ballet? *Paris* – ?

Nana And so I don't exhaust my tolerance for the French and their cooking, once a year, Doctor Jakes and I have agreed to switch places –

Jakes The girls will be very well taken care of, Professor, I promise.

Gum And Petrova?

Jai I've rented a house near my garage for Petrova, Sylvia and me –

Gum And who are you?

Jai Jai –

Gum Jai – ?

Sylvia He's my husband, Gum. We were married this morning.

Whoops and cheers from the household, except –

Gum Married?! Why would you go and do a silly thing like that – ?!

Nana (*warning*) Professor –

Gum Sylvia, you inspired the greatest scientific discovery since the Megalosaurus! I thought you might use it to pursue a career in palaeontology – !

Sylvia I want to be an artist, Gum –

Gum An artist – ?

Sylvia Specifically – a scientific illustrator –

Gum And once I have a moment to process all this change – I'm sure I'll be thrilled for you, but –

Sylvia Gum, I understand this is a lot to take in, but Pauline and Posy have trains to catch and then a boat to meet –

Nana Imminently –

Sylvia So now really isn't the time –

Gum Time – time – there's never enough time, Sylvia – all we have is one-second-hand tick on a giant aeonian clock –

Nana (*looking at her watch*) Professor –

Gum And you and your . . . husband –

Jai Jai –

Gum Jai – have decided how to spend your precious tickety-tock – Pauline and Posy seem intent on theirs – (*Re: Theo.*) and you . . . I still have genuinely no idea who you are –

Theo I'm Theo, / Miss Theo Dane . . .

Posy That's Theo – !

Pauline She taught each of us how to dance.

Theo I'm the new Head of a Children's Stage Academy –

More whoops and cheers.

Gum That's *wonderful*, my dears – *but what about Petrova?* Has anyone asked Petrova what she wants to do – ?

Sylvia Of course we have . . .	**Nana** That train isn't going to wait for us –

Gum Petrova. Forget about everyone else for a moment. Think only of yourself. If you could live anywhere, anywhere in the world . . . where would that be?

Petrova Croydon.

Beat.

Gum Croydon. As in Croydon, South London, England –

Petrova Croydon has the busiest airport in the world.

Gum I see.

Petrova Lots of aeroplanes that need building or flying or fixing.

Gum Well . . . I'd quite like to stay in the same place for a while. And if my family is going to be scattered around the globe, it would certainly help if one of the children trained as a pilot –

Petrova (*thrilled*) Gum – !

Sylvia But where will you both live?

Gum I'll buy a house near the aerodrome –

Sylvia How? You've already been declared legally dead –

Gum I'll go to court. Prove my own existence –

Sylvia And what if you decide to go away on another interminable fossil-hunting expedition – ?

Jai Sylvia . . .   **Nana** Sylvia . . .

Gum Sylvia, I understand my habit of leaving for extended periods of time makes me an unlikely caretaker, but if Petrova will have me –

Petrova I do.

Gum Then I promise, now, to stay consistently by her side.

Petrova and Gum, aligned, stare at Sylvia . . . willing her to agree.

Sylvia Are you sure this is what you want, Petrova?

Petrova Yes. Or to try it . . . at least?

Sylvia (*to Jai*) I suppose . . . I suppose we could go away on a quick honeymoon –

Jai Of course we can –

Gum Of course you can! Pack a few paintbrushes and a pickaxe, jump on a train, and enjoy a quick Jurassic Coast honeymoon-painting-dig, reassured the child has a healthy safety net should I prove a dead or inadequate parent –

Sylvia We'll be back in two weeks, Petrova. And when I say two weeks, Gum, I mean *two weeks* –

Petrova (*hugging her*) We'll be fine, Garnie.

Jai (*handing Gum the key*) I'm leaving my car in your hands, Professor. Please, try not to damage it.

Gum I'm leaving my niece in yours, Jai. I trust the same.

They shake hands.
Then, a moment between Gum and Sylvia.

Gum Goodbye, Mrs . . . (*To Jai.*) Sorry, uh . . . I don't actually know what your last name is –

Sylvia It's Fossil, actually . . .

Jai Mr and Mrs Fossil.

They move to kiss but –

Nana Right! No time for goodbyes – Pauline – Posy – if you want to catch your respective boats – everyone to the station – NOW!

The household files out. The girls stay to make a final vow.
Sylvia lingers a moment to watch them, before leaving also.

Pauline We three Fossils . . .

Posy We three Fossils . . .   **Petrova** We three Fossils . . .

Pauline No matter how old, or busy, or famous, or tired, or important we get, or if we have husbands . . .

Posy Or we don't . . .

Pauline Or children . . .

Petrova Or we don't . . .

Pauline Whether there is a desert, a jungle, a mountain range, an ice belt, a glacial ravine, or an ocean between us . . . we three Fossils vow to remain sisters . . . always.
  We vow.

Posy We vow.

Petrova We vow.

Everyone leaves . . . off on their own adventures . . .
Gum and Petrova clamber into an overpacked car, where luggage competes with a few prized fossils and skeletons for space.

Gum (*to Petrova*) Shall we?

Petrova Bye, house . . .

Gum Did Jai ever tell you, Petrova? This car . . . it's a little bit magic. It can take you wherever you want to go, the emerald-green valleys of Wales, the shimmering mountain lochs of Scotland –

Petrova Croydon Aerodrome, please –

Gum Onwards to Croydon! (*Donning his protective goggles.*) Brace yourself, Petrova; we're set for a thrilling forty-five minutes . . . on the A23 . . .

Gum drives them both towards their new home – ideally, right through the middle of their old one . . . which disassembles, disappears.
Leaning out of the car, Petrova casts a hesitant look back . . . but the roar of an overhead engine draws Petrova's gaze skyward. She stares up, filled with awe and ambition.
Both the house and the car vanish from view.
Beneath the ground, the cherished relics remain . . . safe . . . waiting to be discovered . . . theatre, ballet and aeroplanes . . . now part of the vast, fragmented, discontinuous history of the world.
End of play.

BOWS

A sequence led by Theo, now Head of the Children's Academy.

Everyone has a chance to dance – a showcase of skill, but also of silliness and joy.

At the end, the entire ensemble completes a beautiful révérence, which means, in dance terms: 'Thank you to the stage manager . . . Thank you to the crew . . . Thank you to my fellow performers . . .'

. . . and finally . . .

'Thank you to you . . . my audience . . . for the honour of your time.'